P9-DDU-302

Ultimate CV

WEST BEND LIBRARY

Ultimate CV

Trade secrets from a
recruitment insider

Rowan Manahan

Vermilion
LONDON

WEST BEND LIBRARY

1 3 5 7 9 10 8 6 4 2

Published in 2010 by Vermilion, an imprint of Ebury Publishing

Ebury Publishing is a Random House Group company

Copyright © Rowan Manahan 2004, 2010

Rowan Manahan has asserted his right to be identified
as the author of this Work in accordance with the
Copyright, Designs and Patents Act 1988.

All rights reserved. No part of this publication may be reproduced,
stored in a retrieval system, or transmitted in any form or by any
means, electronic, mechanical, photocopying, recording or
otherwise, without the prior permission of the copyright owner.

The Random House Group Limited Reg. No. 954009

Addresses for companies within the Random House Group
can be found at www.rbooks.co.uk

A CIP catalogue record for this book
is available from the British Library

The Random House Group Limited supports The Forest Stewardship
Council (FSC), the leading international forest certification organisation.
All our titles that are printed on Greenpeace approved FSC certified paper
carry the FSC logo. Our paper procurement policy can be found at
www.rbooks.co.uk/environment

Printed and bound in Great Britain by
CPI Cox & Wyman, Reading, RG1 8EX

ISBN 9780091929244

Portions of this text were originally published in *Where's My Oasis?*

Copies are available at special rates for bulk orders. Contact the sales
development team on 020 7840 8487 for more information.

To buy books by your favourite authors and register for offers, visit
www.rbooks.co.uk

650.14
M 311

For Marie, Lynn and Jane – my reasons for breathing

Contents

'If you wish to persuade me, you must think my thoughts, feel my feelings, and speak my words.'

Marcus Tullius Cicero

'If I can see the world through John Smith's eyes, I can sell John Smith what John Smith buys.'

Madison Avenue adage

Introduction

You come across a job that sounds perfect for you; you have the appropriate qualifications and *oodles* of relevant experience. You dust off your CV and apply and then . . . nothing.

You don't get called to interview. Worse yet, you never hear back from the company in any form, so you have no idea what, if anything, you did wrong.

Someone, in their infinite wisdom, has decided to file your CV in the circular filing cabinet rather than putting you through for interview. Why? Why do so many CVs end up in the bin?

I read application forms, cover letters and CVs every day – some for career management and out-placement clients and many, many more when I am sitting in the hiring chair working on behalf of a client company. I can tell you, in a few short words, why your CV didn't make the grade:

**Because someone else
made my life easier than you did.**

Someone else took just a little more time and a little more trouble to pitch their CV just a little bit better than yours . . . so they made it to the shortlist and you did not. I wish there were a blueprint for how to do this; I wish there were hard-and-fast rules. But there isn't and there aren't. There's just common sense, a bit of canniness and meticulous attention to detail.

What is the Ultimate CV? It is the CV that gets you an interview for *this* job. Not the next job, or the one after that, *this* one. There is a mysterious power in the written word and, as a result, people seem to have difficulty in tampering with anything they have written. In the past, that was understandable – editing clay tablets, letters carved in stone or an illuminated Biblical manuscript must have been very daunting. But now? Select, delete, overwrite, save. What's the problem? So, the Ultimate CV is a fluid, evolving and, above all, *relevant* document – relevant to the reader, the person who has the power to shortlist you and hire you.

Thus, the CV that got you shortlisted for a job in Company X last month may not get you shortlisted for a similar job in Company Y – because Company Y is different. Different management style, different cash-flow issues, different training policy, different marketing philosophy and, most importantly of all, a *different approach to hiring talent.* The Ultimate CV recognises and respects those differences – and that is why you will get shortlisted more often using this approach.

Fundamentally, this is about understanding the mindset of the person who is doing the hiring. I have long maintained that the term 'Screening and Selection' is a misnomer and that the process should be called 'Screening and Elimination'.

Any advertised position in a half-decent company is going to attract a good number of applicants, so the early part of the screening process is a numbers game, plain and simple. For example, if I receive a hundred applications for a middle-management job and I intend interviewing eight to ten of the applicants; as I go through my first pass of the pile of CVs, am I *selecting* or am I *eliminating*? It's a numbers game! With no malice in the world, I am looking to dump 90 per cent of those documents in my bin. Your challenge is not to give me a reason to dump yours.

You want to get on to the shortlist? Make my life easier! Be the right candidate for the job – with the right qualifications, the right experience and the right personal attributes. Let me know that you are *madly* keen to work with me. Show me how polished and professional you are. And, finally, let me know that you understand what a gigantic pain in the ass it is to read a pile of 100 CVs – by engineering your document around *my* requirements, *my* concerns and *my* issues.

The Ultimate CV, *your CV*, is a living document right up to the moment you lick the stamp or hit the 'send' button. Keep drafting, fiddling and playing with it; keep canvassing opinion on it, and identify what works for you. If it doesn't work, follow up to find out why and then go back to the drawing board. *That* is how you write the Ultimate CV.

Top athletes at the pinnacle of their sport spend hours and hours every day working on the basics. How often do you reckon Yo-Yo Ma takes a week – or even a *day* – away from his cello? What about Tiger Woods? Making it to the top 10 per cent of anything in this life is difficult, really difficult. But, every time your CV goes out to speak on your behalf, you are asking it to outstrip 90 per cent of the competition.

Let's make sure it has the best chance to do so . . .

'I do not feel obliged to believe that the same Lord who has endowed us with sense, reason and intellect has intended us to forgo their use.'

Galileo Galilei

Chapter 1

WHY DO SO MANY CVs END UP IN THE BIN?

It is a very unusual job-hunt indeed in which you do not have to produce a written representation of yourself and put it forward, at some stage of the process, to a total stranger. The *curriculum vitae* (or résumé) has to do a very tricky job – it has to catch the reader's attention and then hold that attention by speaking loudly and clearly on your behalf to people who don't care one whit about you. And you will not be there to correct any little misconception or incorrect inference that the reader may draw from your document. There may be some minor thing on your CV that you could clear up in *two seconds* if only you were there – but you're not. So, it is no surprise to discover that:

UGLY FACT NO. 1
NINE OUT OF TEN CVs END UP IN THE BIN

Why does this happen? Even allowing for the fact that a certain number of applicants for every position are just not suitable (irrelevant or insufficient experience, underqualified for the role, lacking key personal attributes, or just plain chancing their arm), that still leaves a significant percentage of solid candidates with relevant track records who end up in the bin at this first stage of the recruitment process.

Why?

If you are suitably qualified, have experience that is immediately pertinent to the positions for which you are applying, but you are not getting invited to interview, then you are either pitching yourself out of your league or your CV is simply not doing its job. Your decision to apply or not to apply for a given job and the quality of the written representation of yourself that you put forward are two aspects of the job-searching process over which you have total control.

That is worth stating again, loud and clear – *that you totally control.*

I recommend that you take the time and trouble to fully exercise that control. But, in doing so, do not make the mistake that so many candidates make of including everything about yourself on your CV. It may be important or seem fascinating to you, but the simple fact is that *no* recruiter cares about your life story at this early stage of the process. Therefore, you need to trim that written representation of yourself to just one or two pages and make damn sure that it *grabs* the reader's attention.

UGLY FACT NO. 2
A BUSY RECRUITER WITH A LARGE PILE OF CVs TO WADE THROUGH IS SIMPLY GOING TO SCAN EACH ONE FOR 15–30 SECONDS

With no malice intended, a recruiter is looking for a reason to dump you in the bin and, if you have not sold yourself in the first 30 seconds, that is where your CV (and, by extension, you) will end up. No one has the time or inclination to plough through three, four or five pages of your professional history and education when they might have another 30, 100 or 500 documents to read after yours. (The exceptions to this are academic, scientific and medical CVs, which can run to 30, 40 or even 50 pages of publications and references.)

RULE NO. 1
YOUR CV IS NOTHING MORE THAN A 30-SECOND ADVERTISEMENT TO GET YOU INVITED TO INTERVIEW

Your CV should be as tightly written as the funniest and cleverest 30-second television advertisement you have ever seen, because 30 seconds is, at most, all your CV will get in which to sell you. If you were spending thousands of pounds to buy 30 seconds of prime-time television airtime to sell yourself to a potential employer, think how carefully you would choose every word. Seriously, try it. 'You should hire me because I . . .' in 30 seconds or less. (This is sometimes known as the 'Elevator Sales Pitch'. The term was coined in Hollywood and means that, if you bump into someone important in the elevator, you have those few moments, while they are trapped in there with you, to make your pitch.)

Accordingly, keep your written representation short, relevant and easy to whiz through. Your CV should reassure the reader of three things and three things only:

- Yes, I can do this job. THIS job, not just any job, but *this* one
- Yes, I am a highly motivated person
- Yes, I will add value to your organisation

In order to be able to write in this way, you need to follow Rule No. 2.

RULE NO. 2
WHEN WRITING ABOUT YOURSELF, THINK LIKE AN EMPLOYER, NOT LIKE A JOB-HUNTER

The poor unfortunate who has to plough through the large pile of CVs has a checklist of desirable experience, qualifications, training and personal attributes. If you can get yourself into that person's head and catch a glimpse of that list, it is much simpler to write the CV that will get you noticed.

'If you can't explain it simply, you don't understand it well enough.'

Albert Einstein

Chapter 2

FOUNDATIONS

ALL OF YOUR HISTORY

To begin the process of compiling your CV, write down everything about yourself, including the associated dates. Do this on your PC so you can edit and amend it over time. You may need to brainstorm with others in order to dredge up all the data and, to start with, just do this as a data-dump; you can put shape and order on it later:

- Your career objectives – short-, medium- and long-term
- A 60-word profile of yourself (the Elevator Sales Pitch, see page 8)
- Companies/institutions/organisations that you have worked for and their locations
- What each organisation did, provided or made and for whom
- Your boss/manager's titles for each of your jobs
- All of your job titles over the years
- Responsibilities and key functions of your jobs
- Promotions or extra responsibilities – why did you get them? Think about the job of work you

were hired to do on day one and the full range of responsibilities you had as you left the organisation (see Appendix 2, page 159)

- Achievements on the job – any time you made a difference. This is frequently the most difficult information to dredge up, but remember that *this* is the reason people will want to meet you. We shall delve into the detail of your accomplishments and contributions with a formal Profiling exercise in Chapter 7; for now, get the big, news-headline stuff down

- Education – full-time, part-time, distance learning. Include your results and qualifications here too

- Training – in-house, formal training with external organisations, and self-directed efforts

- Interests and extra-curricular activities (restrict this to current activities; unless you were a national champion at something, this needs to be up to the minute)

- Achievements off the job – anything interesting from your life outside of work

SECTIONS AND HEADINGS

Now you can decide on your sections and headings: **Professional Progression**, for example, sounds much more impressive than **Work Experience**, but would be an inappropriate heading for a series of summer jobs on a student's CV. You will find language to help you best describe the sections of your CV in Appendix 1 (page 143).

Next, decide the general order of your sections and whether you will place the items within them in chronological or reverse chronological order. When you complete that, you will have the bones of a core *curriculum vitae*, which will be the foundation of all of your applications.

Your core CV will be amended for every job for which you apply. As you identify each new organisation, you will almost certainly need to do some tailoring of your CV and cover letter before applying. No two CVs you send out will contain exactly the same information. It's the same **you** with the same history from document to document, so there may be 80, 90 or even 95 per cent crossover in the information you put forward, but it's those tiny variations that will make the difference.

So, what do you include and what do you omit from your CV each time you send it out?

THE 'SO WHAT?' RULE

The best guideline on this is to read each sentence in your written application from a potential employer's perspective and apply the 'So What?' Rule. Imagine that you are the busy employer/recruiter who is reading the document for the first time. You don't know the writer, you have never heard of the organisations they have worked for and you are not interested in their prowess at Scrabble. At the end of each line or sentence, say, 'So What?'

In other words, 'Why is this applicant telling me this? Does this information make my job of building a shortlist any easier? Does this statement apply to the job that I am trying to fill?' If you cannot adequately answer these questions for any item that appears on your CV, delete it.

A question I am *constantly* asked is: **'I have been working for over XX years now and I just can't get my CV shorter than 3–4 pages. What should I do?'**

Presuming that you have not been in the same role for all those years, and further presuming that you are applying for a comparable or more senior role to your current one, read each sentence in your CV from a recruiter's perspective and *vigorously* apply the 'So What?' Rule.

Too many CVs are nothing more than a restatement of a series of job descriptions. In most instances, the job title tells the reader most of what they need to know about that period of your career. Don't waste space and the reader's time going into minute details. Give them the news headlines about previous positions – title, boss's title, special responsibilities, promotions, contributions that you made and/or what you took from the job.

Anything more than five or six years old is virtually irrelevant in today's market and should be reduced to a line or two. The reader is going to focus on what you are doing *now* and the responsibilities and accomplishments associated with that position, so you should put the bulk of your effort (and space) into that.

Next, you need to decide what *kind* of CV you are going to use.

> 'We are what we repeatedly do. Excellence, therefore, is not an act, but a habit.'
>
> Aristotle

Chapter 3

TYPES OF CV

CHRONOLOGICAL

The most common format used. This CV highlights your career starting from your earliest job and leads up to today, clearly demonstrating your progression along the way. Most people use a Reverse Chronology in their CV, putting the most recent information at the beginning of the document and working their way back through their professional and educational history.

Upside

This is the format most employers expect to see and it is relatively simple to write. It is the best format to use if you are moving within your sector, and has the selling advantage of highlighting both your job titles and the organisations that you have worked for along the way.

Downside

All too often, chronological CVs start to look like autobiographies – too long, too much 'telling' and not enough 'selling'. This kind of CV also makes it hard for you to break out of your pigeon-hole if you are thinking of changing career path. It is also of limited value to you if you are applying for your first job or have a patchy employment history.

FUNCTIONAL

This style of CV highlights your major skills, clustering your achievements and contributions regardless of when they occurred. For example, you may have done a small amount of account handling in three different jobs in your past; the functional style allows you to clump all of the skills and experiences relating to those disparate times into one section of your CV.

Upside

Functional CVs are useful if you have a stop–start history of employment, or if you are trying to highlight particular activities that you want to undertake in your next job. They can also be useful if you are applying either for positions in a new sector or for your first job.

Downside

Because it is a less common format than the chronological CV, the reader may look askance at your application and wonder what you are trying to hide. Human Resources people in particular tend to shy away from wanting to meet candidates who apply in this way.

COMBINATION

This format takes the best elements of the Chronological and Functional CVs, underscoring your major skills within the usual chronological flow. This is a potent combination and, if you discipline your writing style, it can be a real winner.

Upside

Selling all the way.

Downside

The CV can start to run a little long, if you are not very careful. This can be OK for senior roles, but is catastrophic for middle management and below.

TEXT ONLY

Many job sites require that you have a text-only CV and some employers will only accept CVs as part of the text of your email rather than as an attachment.

Upside

Having a text-only version of your CV ready to go will put you ahead of the posse, as most candidates rely on sending a formatted, word-processed document.

Downside

It is difficult to make a text-only document easy to read and, without any formatting, it is also more difficult to highlight the key elements of your professional life to the reader.

ONLINE

The first thing many people do now, when they are about to meet someone for the first time in a professional setting, is to search them in Google. What do people find when they Google you? Well, if you search "rowan manahan" on Google (or Yahoo, Bing or any other search engine), the front page of results will include my blog, my company, my Amazon listings, some stuff from YouTube, my presentations on SlideShare and my online CV. You'll find my online CV, as with so many other people's, on **Linkedin.com**; if you're not already registered there, I highly recommend that you do so straight away.

The trick to controlling your online presence is . . . well, to control it. I'm lucky in that I have an unusual name, but the majority of hits that you get when you search "rowan manahan" are pages that are within my control. So vanity-Google yourself and see what pops up. If it's sparse, then I suggest putting up an online CV on Linkedin, or a similar site. If there's lots of stuff about you, make sure it reflects well on you and start tidying up any old, immature or just plain silly material that's out there.

Upside

Having your CV up on a site like Linkedin means that you are instantly findable – and that site is heavily mined by headhunters and recruiters – but, additionally, it allows you to build a far-reaching online network. You can choose to limit this to intimates – people of whom you have direct knowledge and whom you know and trust sufficiently to show a visible connection to them to the world. Or you can broaden your network to include trusted contacts of your trusted contacts. They can all see your CV (depending on the completeness of your profile and on your privacy settings) and you can also ensure that you appear in searches when employers and recruiters are looking for people with your skillset and background.

Downside

There are obvious Big Brother concerns with having a strong online presence (the terms and conditions on most social networking sites make for truly scary reading). You also need to be careful about how public you are with your online brethren about the fact that you are job-hunting. Your current boss could stumble across a careless status update on Facebook with embarrassing results . . .

BESPOKE

The CV that you write for one specific reader. Typically, this document will be the result of a great deal of meticulous research. You will be writing in the full knowledge of that reader's needs and concerns and presenting yourself as a defined solution rather than just as another potential employee: 'I am the answer to your prayers . . .'

Upside

In a word, potency. If you are well-matched to the organisation's needs and you do the spadework, this form of CV is compelling. Applying this way, via the right person, can get you an interview even if you are lacking in one of the stated requirements for the job.

Downside

There are no downsides to this method, except the wish that you had the time and resources to do this for every application you make . . .

THE ORDER OF SECTIONS ON YOUR CV

The other aspect of the 'So What?' Rule (see page 13) relates to the order in which you place the various sections on your CV. If you are just leaving formal education or if you have just completed a course of study as an adult that is leading you down a new career path, then by all means put your education section first. Otherwise, the reader is interested in seeing two things and two things only for the first pass:

1. **A thumbnail profile of you that tells him immediately if you are in the ballpark for this job**
2. **What you are doing *right now***

Your education, training, contact details and hobbies can all come later in the document.

In my experience, career objective statements are largely worthless and should only be used by those going for their first job; after that, your profile and experience should immediately tell the reader what your story is . . .

In all cases, you should *not* have a frontispiece on your CV – you know the sort of thing I mean:

ROWAN MANAHAN

CURRICULUM VITAE

House Name,
Street Address,
Town,
Postcode.

This is a pointless waste of paper and space. *Of course* it's your *curriculum vitae*! *Du-uh!* What else was it going to be? Simply jump straight in and bring the reader with you:

ROWAN MANAHAN

PROFESSIONAL PROFILE

- Strategic, innovative Career Management professional with a track record of success from entry level to boardroom.
- Demonstrable counselling, analytical, presentation and writing skills.
- Experience gained with job-hunters at all levels, coupled with extensive recruitment work on behalf of corporate and public service organisations.

By the time the reader is a few lines down the page, he should be thinking, 'This candidate is in the ballpark.' All of your efforts in compiling your CV should be directed towards achieving this outcome.

> 'I cannot write five words but that I change seven.'
>
> Dorothy Parker

Chapter 4

THE GRADUATE CV

If you are leaving university (or formal education at another level) for the first time, you should order your CV as follows:

1. Name
2. Education (most recent first, and *briefly* include results/thesis)
3. Work experience (in reverse chronological order)
4. Relevant skills
5. Extra-curricular activities
6. Referees (usually just 'Available upon request')
7. Contact details

In many ways, the first CV you produce is the hardest. It is when you have the least experience, history and self-knowledge at your disposal to distinguish yourself from your peer group. It is for that reason that I counsel that you avoid *any* sort of templated approach like the plague. If you are sending the CV to any of the 'big' companies, they will have seen any template you can find thousands of times before. Take some time, crawl to any of your friends who have design skills and make the look and feel of your document original.

EDUCATION

What distinguishes one, say, electrical engineering graduate from another in the eyes of the reader? You may have completed a minor thesis or project on some aspect of electronics that is relevant to the reader's business, or possibly you took some elective classes that clearly demonstrate your interest in the area to which you are applying. Otherwise, your education section is not much of a differentiator. Sorry.

The exception to this is if you are someone with a brain the size of a planet, who won every scholarship and came first in your class every year since you turned five. Most readers will then sit up and take notice. Otherwise, the beautifully produced page of educational accomplishments on your CV can be reduced to three words in the eyes of the reader: **electrical engineering graduate**. Sorry.

Do try and discover what level of detail individual employers require when it comes to your education section: some will want details of scores of every major exam since the age of 15; some will just want two or three lines about your degree. My overall advice is to *pare it back* because, with the exception of jobs in the groves of academe, no one is interested in the detail of your education.

EXPERIENCE

A summer job that you took just to get more beer money is now going to be scrutinised under a *microscope*. An internship with an organisation in your desired sector would be nice to have, but it can also raise questions such as why you are applying to another company now. Did you not get invited back? Did you not like (or fit in with) the corporate culture and decide not to return? What do either of those outcomes now say about you? The focus of your writing in this section must be on *what you learnt* from the jobs that you have done and, more importantly, *what you contributed* to those employers. Were you in any way special? Did you in any way stand out?

- **Rank** yourself against your peers under every heading you can think of (see The Profiler, page 49)
- What did your customers, suppliers, colleagues and bosses really **think of you?**
- Were you placed in positions of **trust** – key holder, responsible for valuable inventory, cash handling, security?

- Were any **criticisms** levelled at you?
- What about **praise** and compliments? Again, think about colleagues, customers, suppliers and bosses
- Did you make any **suggestions** that were taken on board?
- Were you assigned **extra** responsibilities?
- Did you **solve** any problems or (again!) at least make valuable suggestions?
- What about contributions in a **team** setting?
- Did you complete tasks/projects working on your own **initiative**?

SKILLS

Once more, it is best to look for feedback here – you may have demonstrated a skill that you think is no big deal and which you therefore wouldn't think to include on your CV, but someone observing you might have thought it was pretty special (see The Profiler, page 49).

- Maturity/sense of responsibility beyond your years
- Customers just *loved* you
- Computer literacy – sorting out problems for colleagues/management
- Clean driving licence

・ A *real* facility with a foreign language
・ A *real* ability to impart information to people
・ Public-speaking or presentation skills, which may have been honed in a debating society or class representative role

EXTRA-CURRICULAR ACTIVITIES

I cover these in some depth in Chapter 12 on Application Forms but, at graduate level, the key things we are looking for are:

- Accomplishment
- Initiative
- Leadership potential
- Communication skills
- The ability to work with others

I was a Rubik's Cube expert, a Frisbee coach and a martial arts champion and instructor while I was in secondary school and college. Not exactly run-of-the-mill sports, I grant you, but I was a winner and an achiever in all of these things. When I left college, *all* of my interviews focused in part on what I had had to do to achieve the things I did in those wacky sports, and you can be sure my answers painted me in a positive light. So, as long as your pastime of choice is legal, and as long as you are good at it, you should think about including it on your CV ('Well, I don't like to brag, but I'm grand champion of the universe at cow-pat tossing').

The other interesting detail I notice on graduate CVs is how calculated some people are in pursuing their extra-curricular activities. They are always the Editor, Auditor, Chairman, Treasurer or Elected Representative of any club/society they get involved with while still in education. It may be that no one else wanted these posts or that the person in question had the other candidates kidnapped or ran a dirty campaign in advance of the elections; one way or another, though, they always seem to end up on top.

These are scary people to find yourself in competition with (I call them bogeymen). There is probably a nature/nurture argument here as to whether these people learn to pursue their goals ruthlessly or if they get it from their mother's milk; but one way or another they *do* start early. And, if I've noticed this trend, you can be sure that the person who is going to be reading your CV has noticed it too . . . You need to look for *your* shining points of brilliance and get them front and centre both on your CV and, later, in the interview.

Bottom line, you need to be able to distinguish yourself from your peers in the eyes of the reader. That means that you really have to know what makes your peers tick and what makes you tick. Remember the massive job that your CV is doing here – it is taking the reader from an 'Oh no, not another damn CV' mindset, to curious, to making a decision to set aside some time to meet the writer. If you have ever been in the hiring seat, how many times have you ever done that out of all the applications that have crossed your desk? So, when you are applying at this level, *distinguish*, *reassure* and then *persuade* – that is your order of business. This is all about positioning yourself in the reader's mind. Get into that reader's headspace and give him/her a reason to arrange a get-to-know-you meeting with you.

> 'Experience – that most brutal of teachers.
> But you learn, my God, do you learn.'
>
> C. S. Lewis

Chapter 5

THE UNDER 10 YEARS' EXPERIENCE CV

This ordering of sections on your CV will be useful in the early stages of your career. You could put education up front if you have just completed a significant course of study that pertains better to the role you are applying for than your current job does. Otherwise, you are better off starting with a brief profile and jumping straight into your current role.

1. Name
2. At a glance
3. Career and achievements
4. Education (always most recent first)
5. Training and relevant skills (always most recent first)
6. Professional memberships
7. Extra-curricular activities
8. Referees (on request)
9. Contact details

CAREER AND ACHIEVEMENTS

The achievements or contributions section is the part you really need to spend time on. This is the transferable stuff that employers will want to talk about at interview. You don't need to get too far into the '**how**' of your achievements; focus instead on the '**what**' – this will invite 'how' questions at the interview, which in turn will allow you to start really selling yourself.

You rarely need to get into the minute details of your job description and areas of responsibility. For example, if you are a Management Accountant, a simple phrase along the lines of 'In addition to the usual responsibilities' immediately enables you to delineate the special or expanded responsibilities that you have sought out or that have been devolved to you.

Every professional CV reader knows the 'usual suspects' list of responsibilities, so don't take up a lot of space on these, particularly for older jobs. To help you to do this, complete the exercise in Appendix 2 (page 159) for each job you have held. This will quickly show how, or if, you developed within the role in each position. Here is one way of laying this out:

• Last point of your professional profile

CAREER & ACHIEVEMENTS

AUGUST 200X TO PRESENT

Headhunted by *Widgets Incorporated (UK)* as **Management Accountant,** reporting to the Financial Controller. *Widgets* competes in the blah-blah sector, the local affiliate has a turnover of £XX million and has 350 staff. My brief encompasses:

• Preparation of monthly/quarterly/annual accounts and variance-based reporting
• VAT analysis and reporting
• Cash flow reporting
• Liaising with banks, suppliers and debtors
• Ongoing liaison with auditors and regulatory authorities

Special responsibilities:

• Development, implementation and updating of all policies and procedures within my purview
• Capital Expenditure projects from inception to completion (£ amount)
• Collaboration on key projects – insurance, systems development, stock control

Contributions:

• Migration from legacy system to SAP – project team member
• Merger, Acquisition & Diligence activities from time to time
• Conducting training in Finance for non-financial management

EDUCATION

A simple and clean way of presenting this information is in a table. You should work in reverse chronological order and only include those details that will be of interest to the reader. Once you are a few years out of education, no one really cares what subjects you took in second year or what results you got – unless it was something ferociously impressive.

• Last point of your career and achievements section

EDUCATION

INSTITUTION	QUALIFICATION	YEAR
College name, location	**Masters in Business Administration** Thesis: Implementing an ERP System in the multinational setting	2010
Institute name, location	**Membership Exams (ACA)**	2005
School name, location	**A Levels**	2001

Make the table lines invisible and it is even easier to read:

• Last point of your career and achievements section

EDUCATION

INSTITUTION	QUALIFICATION	YEAR
College name, location	**Masters in Business Administration** Thesis: Implementing an ERP System in the multinational setting	2010
Institute name, location	**Membership Exams (ACA)**	2005
School name, location	**A Levels**	2001

TRAINING AND RELEVANT SKILLS

A *very* important section. Training represents the investment *in you* made by your current and past employers; so, if they aren't making that investment, it will be setting off alarm bells in the reader's head . . . This is why it is vital to put yourself forward for any training that is available within your organisation. You don't want to sound whiny and needy to your boss, but make sure she is aware of your commitment to personal development and lifelong learning.

'Job security' and 'take-home pay' have been listed as the two key drivers/motivators for employees in all the workplace studies conducted since World War II – until recently that is. The latest studies are showing that ongoing training and development has supplanted job security, no doubt because employees have recognised that job security is an extinct concept. If your employer is not developing you and investing in you, beware. It is the career management equivalent of strip mining – it looks bad on your CV, but, more importantly, it means that your skillset is becoming outdated.

You should present the training section on your CV in the same way as education – in an easy-to-read, tabular format.

One other thing about training: just because you have been sent on a training course doesn't necessarily mean that you have to include it on your CV, particularly if the training has no relevance for this new employer or if it has been in any way 'corrective' (this would be especially true if you have been sent on training following an unfavourable appraisal).

MEMBERSHIPS

List your professional memberships by way of reassurance, but also because your new employer will usually be picking up the tab for them.

'When people are free to do as they please, they usually imitate each other.'

Eric Hoffer

Chapter 6

THE EXECUTIVE/SENIOR CV

For these, the order of the sections should be as follows:

1. Name
2. Professional profile
3. Key accomplishments (I have found it best to split these up and tailor them as appropriate for each application)
4. Professional progression (focus heavily on promotions and achievements. If length is not a problem, you can give some detail of 'how' you made these things happen)
5. Education and accreditations (most recent first)
6. Other training and relevant skills
7. Professional memberships
8. Extra-curricular activities
9. Referees (on request)
10. Contact details

These CVs are always the most difficult to write and, as you get older, involve an agonising process of compression – which elements do you omit altogether and which do you highlight? An effective CV for a senior player in any sector is going to be dependent on heavy research and very tight positioning. There's more at stake here and the return on investment is far larger, so executives typically enlist help from a professional CV-crafting service. My advice on this is to shop around and, if possible, to select your wordsmith on the basis of a referral from someone you know and trust. The really good ones will offer a 'no quibble' policy – if you are not completely happy with the end result, you don't have to pay anything.

'How long or short should it be?' is the question that most senior executives think about when it comes to representing themselves in writing. My answer, as always, is, 'That depends.'

First, it depends on how well-known you are. In the unlikely event that he was applying for a job, Mr Paul Hewson's CV could consist of the words, 'Howerya, I'm Bono.' He is a brand – instantly recognisable, memorable and indelibly associated with the work and events with which he has been involved. You may not have *quite* this degree of fame, but you might be very well-known to some of the people that you are going to be writing to, in which case brevity will serve you well. Detail your history and your major accomplishments without delving too much into the 'how' of those accomplishments.

If, however, you are a relative unknown, you will need to provide more reassurance to the reader. Remember the enormous task that your CV is doing here – it is taking the reader from a neutral mindset to curious, to genuinely interested, to making a decision to set aside time from a busy schedule to meet the person behind the pages. Think how *rarely* that happens.

Most CVs end up in the bin, and with good reason. When you are applying at this level, you need to tailor the information to *inform* the reader of the big events of your career and, if you have made them relevant to his situation, he will be *persuaded* and will set up an appointment. No one is going to hire you purely on the basis of your excellent CV but, if your CV is less than excellent, no one is going to bring you to the next stage of the process.

So, you are a Bono. You're very well-known in your sector and your reputation precedes you. I contend that you still need an outstanding CV simply because, 99 times out of 100, you are going to be viewed by people (board members, non-executive directors, management outside of your area of expertise, young recruitment consultants) who have never heard of you and in the context of a bunch of other people with a similar background putting themselves forward for the same job. So, take the time, do the hard analysis, do the soul-searching and get the document glittering!

LENGTH

Most professionals should be able to condense the juicy bits of their working lives down to about two pages. Some like to keep it to a one-page résumé, but that is very hard to do, both in terms of content and in look and feel, and you will definitely need professional help to achieve this.

My guideline for senior players is to spend 50 per cent of your space detailing the last five to seven years, or your last two jobs. Jobs from further back in your history can be reduced to a few lines – one or two big highlights only. No one is going to be interested in your early history other than to get a sense of the rapidity of your progression and the scope of the roles you had; unless you have had a highly unorthodox early career, I would recommend presenting the early stuff in a space-saving table:

JOB TITLE	COMPANY	DATES
Head of Marketing	Wonder Inc.	1999-01
Sales & Marketing Manager	Chunder Inc.	1996-99
Sales Manager	Thunder Ltd. (secondment)	1995-96
Product Manager	Thunder Ltd.	1991-95
Marketing Executive	Blunder Inc.	1989-91

And then provide detail of your challenges, changes and accomplishments for your last two roles – in this instance, Sales & Marketing Director and Managing Director – which encompass the last 10 years. If you are going for a head of function role or a General Manager/Managing Director role, no one is going to care about the detail of your time way back as a Sales or Product Manager. Yes, the skills and knowledge that you gained back then are central to your success since, but they have little or no applicability, under the 'So What?' Rule, to your application for an MD/GM job.

If there is a seismic event from way back in your career – you launched the all-singing, all-dancing, market-leading product; you came up with the positioning or strategy for some household name item; you invented the global standard auditing system – then, rather than expanding upon that by splitting out a job from 15 years ago, simply highlight it in the Key Accomplishments section on your front page. That way, the reader can say, 'Oh, *she's* the person who came up with the idea of widening the nozzle in the toothpaste tube, thus doubling her company's sales overnight . . .'

TONE

Badly-produced CVs invariably stray too far down the 'telling' road, listing what are essentially a series of job descriptions. But I have also encountered CVs that are all 'sell' and no 'tell'. I can see where these people are coming from – they have to get all the good stuff across and they have limited space, so they ruthlessly edit out anything that doesn't make me raise my eyebrows.

I tend to moderate this 'accomplishments all the way' approach slightly, as it can come across as too self-aggrandising and turn the reader off. A balanced approach – a little delineation of the scope and progression of your role, balanced with a goodly chunk of accomplishment/contribution language – will serve you better in most cases.

The other strand to look out for in the tone of your document is the passive voice:

- Costs were cut by XX per cent over three years
- Sales grew by YY per cent year on year
- And then I ended up . . .

Contrast those with:

- My team reduced costs by XX per cent over three years
- I expanded sales by YY per cent year on year
- I moved to . . . /I was appointed to . . . (rather than 'I ended up . . .')

When I lay out examples like this in seminars, people always look at me as if to say, 'Ah, come on, Robo, I'm not *that* careless and lazy – give me some credit. I would never phrase things that way on my CV.' All I would quietly say in response is that someone would, and is. More than someone – a whole lot of people let the passive voice creep into their written communication. Know it, fear it, root it out, dump it (see CV Thesaurus, page 143).

'There are only two ways of telling the complete truth – anonymously and posthumously.'

Thomas Sowell

Chapter 7

THE PROFILER – THINKING OBJECTIVELY ABOUT YOURSELF

WHY DO I NEED SUCH A ROUNDED VIEW OF MYSELF?

Hold up a pen. Look at it from all sides. Now describe that pen to a person over the phone. This is not difficult – a pen is a simple, familiar object that is well-known to everyone.

Stand a person you know well on a chair. Now describe that person to someone else over the phone. Do it so well that the other person can pick your friend out of a police line-up. Not so easy.

Now describe your friend again, but this time in terms of his or her skills, qualities and unique way of doing things. Try doing that in terms that are relevant to the person on the end of the phone. Try doing that when the person on the other end of the phone has 20 more similarly qualified, similarly experienced people being recommended to her. Hmm . . . tricky.

That is why you need such a clear and rounded view

of yourself as you approach the market. If knowledge is power, then self-knowledge is the most useful force you can wield in your career and any job-hunts you undertake in that career. People who have gained insight into themselves are much more effective leaders, team members and employees, and are valued as such by employers.

It is easy to describe a pen. It is very hard to write about yourself. To condense all of your experiences and accomplishments into a few succinct paragraphs in order to make the reader want to meet you is no laughing matter. We have already talked about all of the data that you need to collate, and about picking the essential components – the elements that address a specific reader's concerns. But a well-written CV is more, much more, than that. A winning CV, one that immediately grabs the reader's attention and pricks her interest, is a CV that gives that reader a flavour for the kind of person you are.

Take it to the next stage and put yourself in the boots of the interviewer. Let's say you have shortlisted 10 candidates for a job. Let's also say that, after a brief phone interview, two of them are revealed to be unprofessional clowns, two are arrogant creeps and the other six seem like reasonably competent, decent people. On probing deeper, you discover that two of the remaining six don't like themselves very much and another two are carrying chips on their shoulders from previous employments.

So, you have whittled it down to the final two – one of whom can talk about himself with great conviction, understands how he is perceived by suppliers, customers, bosses and colleagues and makes sure that he doesn't ruffle feathers with any of those groups, and has gained a reputation (when you do the background check) for having a Midas touch when it comes to dealing with people and getting the best out of them.

The final candidate is similarly qualified, similarly experienced and has a comparable track record of success, but just doesn't provide you with the same level of reassurance on his abilities in dealing with people. The technical term for this kind of hiring situation is A NO-BRAINER.

So do The Profiler. Do it on yourself and then ask other people, whose opinions you value, to fill in the boxes for you. You can offer to do it as a trade with friends and family members or with old colleagues ('I'll show you mine if you'll show me yours . . .').

If you already know all of this juicy stuff about yourself and that it coincides with what the world thinks of you, lucky you (and why are you reading this book?). If you are not *sure* of this knowledge, get to work . . .

THE JOB THAT I DO

Current or most recent job title:

Your boss's title:

Type of organisation:

Key areas of responsibility:

-
-
-
-
-

BREAKDOWN OF CURRENT/MOST RECENT JOB

What I do/did very well in my job (think of third-party evidence here – compliments from co-workers, customers or your boss, for example):

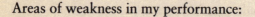

Areas of weakness in my performance:

The best and worst aspects of my job are/were:

ACCOMPLISHMENTS

A professional achievement is something that (a) you did well and enjoyed; (b) made a contribution that could be measured; or (c) would make you interesting to a prospective employer. Examples could include developing a new idea, service, product, process or procedure; exceeding a sales, profit or market-share target; reducing inventory or other costs; improving profit margins; streamlining an important part of your job; making some part of the business more efficient; being assigned to recruit, supervise and/or train other people or being assigned a broader area of responsibility on the job.

Look at the accomplishments you achieved in the past 5–10 years (if it goes back further than that, it will need to be truly earth-shaking stuff). The table below should help you come up with some good material. In each case, indicate exactly what you did, the immediate result and what it meant to your team or organisation in the longer term.

	MY INPUT	IMMEDIATE RESULT	LONG-TERM EFFECT
Turnover or other growth?			
Targets or deadlines met/exceeded?			
New business gained?			
New processes/procedures?			
New product/service/idea?			
Streamlining approach?			
Significant problem(s) solved?			
Cost savings?			

	MY INPUT	IMMEDIATE RESULT	LONG-TERM EFFECT
Special relationships (internal or external) developed or fostered to a new level?			
Recruiting and managing staff?			
Mentoring or assisting new staff?			
Training of new staff?			
Cross-training existing staff?			
Motivating staff with special incentives?			
Staff turnover reduced?			
Any initiatives, suggestions or other contributions?			

Pick the top five to seven accomplishments from your recent years and list them below in order of importance to the organisation you were working for.

1.

2.

3.

4.

5.

6.

7.

ME IN A NUTSHELL
Describe your professional self in one sentence. Imagine that you have just met a headhunter at a party:

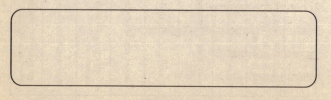

Give yourself marks out of 10
for the following:

Commitment ☐

Urgency ☐

Professionalism ☐

Flexibility/adaptability ☐

Learning curve ☐

Empathy ☐

Finance/numeracy ☐

Writing skills ☐

Selling ☐

People management/motivating ☐

Administration ☐

Dealing with multiple tasks ☐

Crisis management ☐

Event management ☐

Analysis/ability to evaluate ☐

Creativity/innovation ☐

Account management ☐

Fostering relationships/networking ☐

Problem-solving ☐

Interpersonal skills ☐

MY SKILLBASE

Talents are the special abilities that you are born with; *skills* are learnt, honed and developed on an ongoing basis. Reflect on your full range of skills, those used both in and out of work.

IT skills? What packages do you use well?

Recruitment, team-building/training skills?

The following list delves further into your skillset. The skills are broken down into four categories. Give yourself marks out of 10 for **how good you are** at each skill (we will look at the skills that you **enjoy** later; for now, just measure your ability).

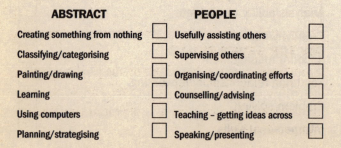

ABSTRACT		PEOPLE	
Creating something from nothing	☐	Usefully assisting others	☐
Classifying/categorising	☐	Supervising others	☐
Painting/drawing	☐	Organising/coordinating efforts	☐
Learning	☐	Counselling/advising	☐
Using computers	☐	Teaching – getting ideas across	☐
Planning/strategising	☐	Speaking/presenting	☐

Under what **constraints** have you operated?
(rank if necessary)

Time ☐

Budget ☐

Targets ☐

Multiple clients ☐

Regulations ☐

Laws ☐

Corporate guidelines/expectations ☐

preference, are you a **team player** or a **solo flyer**?

at is your preferred style in a team setting? (e.g.
der, Explorer, Facilitator, Policeman, Devil's
ocate, etc.)

ou have any experience with quality or auditing
ms – ISO9000, EFQM, TQM, British Standards
nilar?

Teaching – explaining concepts ☐ Negotiating ☐

Researching/finding out new stuff ☐ Listening ☐

Writing ☐ Empathising ☐

Mathematics ☐ Fostering relationships ☐

Exploring/investigating ideas ☐ Selling ☐

INFORMATION

Reading ☐

Working with numbers ☐

Following instructions ☐

Making decisions ☐

Seeing to the heart of the issue ☐

Learning ☐

Noticing important details ☐

Using computers ☐

PHYSICAL

Operating equipment ☐

Driving ☐

Doing mechanical tasks ☐

Cooking ☐

Gross motor skills – sports ☐

Painting and decorating ☐

Using tools ☐

DIY – building/repairing ☐

Can you think of any other core skills you have, other than those already mentioned?

MY TOP SEVEN SKILLS

From the picture you have built on the previous pages, list those skills at which you excel and which you think make you attractive as a potential employee in today's workplace:

1.

2.

3.

4.

5.

6.

7.

Now list the seven skills that you most **enjoy** using, in order of satisfaction:

1.

2.

3.

4.

5.

6.

7.

How closely do the two skill lists correlate? Going back to basics, it is imperative that you pursue a

career that (a) you are **good at,** and (b) yo
You might be the best Widgeting Enginee
planet but, if widgeting leaves you cold,
placing yourself at risk. You are at risk beca
health can suffer as a result of doing work
not fulfil you and you are at risk beca
morale will suffer. Management will noti
they have to make tough choices about w
keep and whom they let go in some futu
turing exercise, your name is unlikely to
the 'keep' or 'promote' list.

MY STYLE

What is your **focus** on the job? (rank 1

Customers

Quality

Profit

Results

Procedures

Winning

Cost control

Productivity

Keeping the team going

Have you been given any particularly positive feedback over the years? From whom?

Any themes emerging in the feedback? Think hard about this – we get a lot of contemporaneous praise in our working lives and, typically, it falls out of our heads five minutes later. Think!

Describe yourself with five adjectives.

1.

2.

3.

4.

5.

What is your most significant professional *weakness*?

MY PERSONAL DEVELOPMENT

List the most useful training courses or programmes that you have ever been on:

COURSE TITLE	INSTITUTION/ COMPANY	YEAR	USEFUL BECAUSE ...

What would you spend a £5,000 **personal** (not technical) training budget on this year?

Best moment in your career/life to date?

How would your best friend describe you?

1.

2.

3.

4.

5.

Why does he or she value you so much?

What about your current boss/co-workers?
(or most recent)

1.
2.
3.
4.
5.

Who was your most difficult boss to work with
and why?

Worst moment in your career/life to date?

Where do you plan to be in your professional life
in five and in ten years' time?

CURRENT INTERESTS

For your CV, you should consider including *current* interests under the following broad headings:

Professional

Membership of trade or other organisations, committee activities, special projects. All of these imply a level of professionalism and commitment to your chosen career.

Physical

Some level of physical activity will reassure the reader that you are not a total slob with all of the associated keeling-over-at-your-desk health risks of slobdom . . .

Cerebral

Do you do anything to improve your mind or keep it active? Reading (tell them what kind of books, papers, magazines), cinema, theatre and music (again, tell them what kind) are all examples of cerebral activities.

Social

Many jobs will require you to talk over food with suppliers and customers, or to work effectively with other people in teams. If you enjoy cooking, have knowledge

of a certain type of food, or anything that demon-
strates an ability and comfort in this area, include it.

Altruistic

If you are involved in fundraising, local charities,
your residents' association, your children's school,
you should mention it (Message: 'I am a decent,
involved human being . . .').

CANVASSING OPINION

So, now you have your viewpoint and, hopefully, you
have discovered a few useful things about yourself.
Time to start getting other people's input on some of
the items – skills, loves and hates, accomplishments,
weaknesses, great moments. *Any* feedback you can
get from someone who knows you well could be
useful.

Remember: their perception is *their* reality. Even if
you vociferously disagree with something that they
point out about you, take it on board. You may not
have intended to behave or be perceived in that way,
or they may have *totally* misconstrued what was
behind your action, but it is real to them and they
have had the courage and courtesy to tell you.
Thank them.

You are looking for points of convergence (and disagreement) here. So, you think you are very empathetic and that you are a good listener, but what do the people in your trusted circle tell you? Does the feedback confirm or deny your assertion? What do you think? What do you know? What can you *prove*?

> 'The greater our knowledge increases, the greater our ignorance unfolds.'
>
> John F. Kennedy

Chapter 8

ME, AT A GLANCE

Another one of those questions I get asked all the time: 'How do you write an introductory profile of yourself? I have heard that putting one of these at the top of my CV will really help my chances of getting to interview, but where do I start? What do I include or leave out?'

Many CVs now come with a profile or thumbnail overview of the candidate at the top. In my experience, too many of these are stale, unsubstantiated, buzzword-driven tripe. This is the kind of stuff I see all the time:

- 'Dynamic, forward-looking sales professional.'
- 'I am a self-starter, brimming with enthusiasm.'
- 'I have highly developed people skills.'
- 'I am a blah-blah-blah, keen to apply my yadda-yadda skills in a blue-chip environment.'

So what? No, really. So bloody what? Look at those statements again from the perspective of a tired recruiter who is wading through a tall pile of applications:

'Dynamic, forward-looking sales professional.'

(a) Says who?

(b) Maybe I don't want a 'dynamic' rep. Maybe I just want someone who keeps her nose to the grindstone and gets on with the job. I want a persistent grafter who won't alienate my customers by spouting this kind of twaddle!

'I am a self-starter, brimming with enthusiasm.'

Well, golly gee willikers, I suspect that, if I meet you, the word 'perky' is going to spring to mind and, if your CV is any indicator, I am probably going to lose my lunch to boot.

'I have highly developed people skills.'

What are you – a contestant in a beauty pageant? I bet you love to travel, and are kind to animals, old people and children too; and your most fervent wish is for world peace . . .

'I am a blah-blah-blah, keen to apply my yadda-yadda skills in a blue-chip environment.'

Guess what, sonny? Everybody else in the pile wants to work here too . . .

ENCAPSULATING YOURSELF

Profiling yourself succinctly should be quite easy. You talk about what you do for a living all the time

– to colleagues, your family, people at parties. But that is usually an **informative** discourse; you are not having to justify your existence *per se*.

A thumbnail sketch at the top of a CV is a **persuasive** discourse. A tight, every-word-included-for-a-reason, selling statement. 'I am *exactly* what you need. I am making your life just a little easier here. Binning me would be a bad idea.' All useful impressions to leave in the reader's mind.

I recommend building a list of about 10 items for possible inclusion in your professional profile. The Profiler (see page 49) should give you lots of ammunition, hopefully more than you need. You probably won't use more than five or six items from this embarrassment of riches for any one application.

But you do need to get them into some kind of shape.

Point 1
Should be your one-liner about yourself. I know what *I* am. I am a **'Strategic, innovative Career Management professional with a track record of success from entry-level to boardroom.'** What are you? Clearly, this point needs to fit closely with their perceived needs. You might need to reach for a thesaurus to make that happen. Some examples could be:

- Strategic financial professional with a strong commercial and development record
- Entrepreneurial senior financial professional currently with a multi-billion-pound company
- Seasoned Chief Executive with broad experience and demonstrable track record of accomplishment
- Blue-chip-trained project management professional with a background in high finance, M&A, green-field, and multi-cultural deals
- Business postgraduate with solid commercial experience gained in a large financial institution

Point 2

A big attention-grabber: 'All sales and market share targets exceeded for the last five years' would probably have been a better line for our Sales Rep above. Now *that* is a person the reader wants to meet. She understands what selling is all about and isn't wasting the reader's time in any way. Other examples could be:

- Comfort in building/changing/restructuring businesses for growth, finance or sale
- Built six key brands to market leadership, exceeding parent company expectations
- Breadth of financial experience includes: IPO, merger, sale of subsidiary and company

- Disciplined programme manager, skilled at bringing teams in a focused direction
- Demonstrable track record in managing complex, pressurised projects with large numbers of participants
- Specialist in financial management and planning for diverse elements of a group
- Proven record of quality, relevant, timely reporting and contribution to robust decision-making and performance management

Clearly, the points above are *very* specifically tailored to positions that the writers have extensively researched. If you know, *really know*, what you are going to be doing in the new job, then pitching your profile to it like this is a cinch. Without that depth of research, you are relying on woolly generalisations and your CV starts to look and smell like junk mail.

Point 3
The big, transferable and relevant (above all, *pleeeease*, relevant) skills. Have they been central to your success? Are they attested to by your referees? Have you enhanced them through training that you mention further on in your CV? Examples could be:

- Excellent analytical, leadership, interpersonal and change-management skills
- Strong event- and crisis-management and media-handling skills
- Exceptional interpersonal, relationship management and presentation skills
- Excellent analytical, reasoning, budgetary, writing and IT capacities
- Strong abilities in recruitment, team-building and training for new and existing staff

Now, if you just stuck these up there cold, they wouldn't have the impact or credibility that you need. But putting them as the third point below a positioning statement and a verifiable 'What I do' grants them a strong foundation.

Point 4
Secondary skills – the competencies you have that get the job done. Your middle of the bell-curve stuff. Again, these should be reverse-engineered from your understanding of what the job that you are applying for entails: 'Comfortable and effective with X, Y and Z.' Some examples are:

- Effective team leadership with an open, collaborative style

- Astute at finding creative, effective solutions within complex environments
- Comfortable relating to technical/non-technical management and staff at all levels
- High degree of computer literacy – familiar and effective with all key applications used by [the company you are applying to]
- Highly developed recruitment, team-building and training skills to positive outcomes
- Reputation gained as a problem-solver with strong strategic, logical and analytical capacities

Point 5

What have you been recognised for? Promoted for? Singled out for? 'Consistently selected to deal with technical/sensitive/intractable deals' would be a nice thing to be able to say if the job you are applying for involves a lot of negotiation. Other examples are:

- Consistently recognised for professionalism, management of complex, integrated projects, teamworking and results
- Recognised by management for acquisition review and corporate finance projects
- Selected by international management to troubleshoot intricate, technical and sensitive projects

- Recognised and promoted throughout my career for my steep learning curve, professionalism and results
- Consistently recognised for innovation, commitment, customer relations and flexibility

Point 6

The clincher. Your focus on the job and the constraints under which you are comfortable working. 'I am not some kind of snot-nosed, starry-eyed naïf here – I know what matters and I understand how the world works.' Thoughts:

- Commercially driven, while working within regulatory and budgetary constraints
- Customer-service and quality-focused, while working to corporate expectations and tight time-frames
- Focused on profitable production within JIT system and to agreed targets
- Customer-focused while working within time, budgetary and legal constraints

BLINDINGLY OBVIOUS STATEMENT

You must be able to support every syllable in your profile, and your referees need to be primed and ready to confirm these statements. I know that it can be very tempting to do so, but you really, really should not overstate the case – there is a *world* of difference between 'Strong', 'Excellent' and 'Exceptional' skills in any capacity.

A well-phrased profile does more than get you to the shortlist; it begins to **set the agenda** for the interview that follows. So don't go claiming that you can walk on water or raise the dead and expect them to breeze past it when you are in the hot seat. You are planting seeds here; be ready for the drill-down that will inevitably follow.

BULLETS OR PARAGRAPHS?

I favour a bullet-point approach to profiling, probably because I spend so much time reading CVs, and also because I am a firm believer that people are lazy dogs and won't take the time to read a four-line paragraph, but they might, just *might*, scan-read five or six tightly composed bullets.

Writing about yourself this way takes a lot of forethought and practice. But, if you do it well, the tired reader will *beam* at you for making his life just a little bit easier, and you are far less likely to end up filed in the bin.

OH, AND ANOTHER THING . . .

I wrote a version of this chapter in 2003 and it was

published in *Where's My Oasis* and also extracted in a couple of places on the internet. And, guess what? I started seeing the *exact language* of some of the bullet points above on CVs shortly afterwards.

The reason I haven't slavishly produced CV templates or a database of handy profile-y points in an accompanying CD-ROM with this book is because, very quickly, anyone who reads CVs for a living will spot that lifted, samey-samey, material.

DO NOT copy other people's words.

Slow down, take your time and write your own. I cannot stress this enough – DO NOT use any CV template or language that you find anywhere. Think about what a lazy-ass template says to the reader, who has seen that layout a thousand times before. Think about what a stolen line says to that reader . . .

> 'Trying to define yourself is like trying to bite your own teeth.'
>
> Alan Watts

Chapter 9

FORMATTING AND DESIGN

Distinguishing yourself from everyone else in a large pile of CVs is no easy matter. **What** you say about yourself is obviously vital, but **how** you present it can also have a large bearing on whether or not you get shortlisted.

Look-and-feel is the first 5 per cent and the last 10 per cent of a well-crafted CV or résumé. It's the first 5 per cent because, when I am wading through a large pile of CVs, it is very hard for me to be professional enough not to throw your CV in the bin if it is in any way hard for me to read. (Have you ever noticed that, while CVs aren't particularly aero-dynamic, they do make a very pleasing fluttering noise as they head towards the bin?)

Look-and-feel is the last 10 per cent because, when I have eliminated all the dross and no-hopers, I pay very close attention to people who have paid very close attention to the details on their CV. The one assumption we can fairly make as hirers is that you **give a damn about yourself**. Therefore, if you have not bothered with attending to the fine detail *on your own* *behalf*, what prospect is there that you will attend to the fine detail on behalf of your new employer?

You wouldn't show up to the bank wearing torn jeans and an 'All Bank Managers Are Bastards!' T-shirt and expect to be taken seriously. In today's market, you need to take the look-and-feel aspects of your written representation of yourself very seriously indeed. Yes, of course, the other 85 per cent matters immensely, but people get screened out on the basis of sloppiness in their written representation just as they get screened out for having scuffed shoes at the interview.

Every aspect of your document needs to be perfect. Layout and styling can only be finalised when you have a specific job to apply for and, no matter what anyone tells you, there are no hard and fast rules for CVs – different people will inevitably like different things. That being said, you won't go far wrong if you follow these eight rules of thumb:

1. WORD-PROCESS IT

Unless you are going for a job as a calligrapher, your CV should be crisply produced on standard word-processing software. If you are stuck with a legacy system or a little-known and not widely used application, save your CVs and letters in Rich Text

Format (filename.rtf). This will allow you to transfer your files between different computers with little or no difficulty.

2. FONTS

Use appropriate typefaces. Word-processing packages these days come with umpteen fonts, the majority of which are worthless for business use; save them for fun activities and use Times or a similar, serif font (serifs are the little tails that finish the strokes of letters; sans serif fonts are cleaner and more modern-looking, but can also be a little soulless). Most of what we read in physical form is produced in serifed fonts – newspapers, magazines and books – and we are accustomed to reading them and believing them.

If your paper CV is likely to be scanned, you may need to use a sans serif font like Arial, Verdana or Gill Sans and test it by OCR (Optical Character Recognition) to assess layout and legibility. Underlining can also cause problems for scanners.

Don't use rare or specialist fonts, particularly if you are going to send soft copies of your CV by email (see below) as the receiving computer may not have those fonts installed and all of your careful formatting will be ruined.

3. LEGIBILITY

Allow generous margins and plenty of white space on your CV – this will make it easier to read. Headings should be 2–3 point sizes larger than your body text and the bulk of your CV should be in a font size no smaller than 11 point. If you are going smaller than that to cram in more information, you should question the utility and impact of every word that you are including. Your font sizes should also contribute to making life easy for the reader:

TIMES 14 BOLD CAPITALS
Times 12 regular
Times 11 regular
Times 10 – getting a little hard to read
Times 8 – way too small – typically used when you need to cram in more information than will comfortably fit

GILL SANS 14 BOLD CAPITALS
Gill Sans 12 regular
Gill Sans 11 regular
Gill Sans 10 – still readable because it's sans serif

There is another issue on font sizes: it doesn't happen often any more, but some recruitment agencies still fax CVs to client organisations, so your layout needs to retain its legibility when it has been sent to a crumbly old fax machine and the lettering becomes fuzzy. Once again, test it and see if it works . . .

4. WALK ON BY

Walk the reader through the document – think about what matters most to them and put that up front (see The Order of Sections for each of the CV types we talked about earlier). Demarcate your sections clearly using headings in a different font (or style) and lines, boxes, shading or white space. For ideas, look at how the text in your favourite newspaper or magazine is laid out or talk to a friend in the design business.

5. PACKAGING

You don't buy products in the supermarket with cheap, dented, torn, rusty or faded packaging and, funnily enough, neither do employers. If you are sending off a printed CV or physically handing one to anybody you meet in your job-hunt, consider the following:

- Use **high-quality paper** with a weight of 100 grams or heavier. Don't 'liberate' 80-gram paper from the photocopier at work: invest in a ream or two of decent paper for your job search. Human beings are fundamentally tactile and, while you won't get any extra marks for using good stationery, if you don't, it can indicate a less-than-professional approach.

- Print everything at **high resolution** (600 dpi) on a laser printer. Some of the latest inkjets also print text quite well – if you have one, experiment with different resolutions on different papers until you are happy.

- **Don't photocopy** your CV for submission, unless you have access to a professional photocopier the size of a bus. (Anyway, why do you need dozens of copies of your CV? You are going to be tailoring it for each application you make.)

- If you are posting hard copies, send your CV flat (not folded) in a crisp, **white, A4 envelope**.

- Print your **address label** or envelope. Handwrite your return address clearly.

- Buy your own **stamps**; do not frank your envelopes at work. The reader *will* check and it *is* theft.

6. BINDERS

I am amazed that I still have to give this piece of advice but, if you are submitting a hard copy of your CV by post, *do not bind it*! Binders are just a nuisance and always get torn off and thrown in the bin, to the accompaniment of a lot of irritation on the part of the reader. Binders make reading, photo-copying, scanning and filing your CV more difficult, so *don't*. A paperclip or staple is perfectly sufficient.

If you are neurotic (like me) you can use a clear plastic slip cover – the kind that opens on two sides. (When I was in primary school, I firmly believed that you got an extra 5 per cent if you handed in your homework in one of these. If only life were still that simple.)

7. SOFT COPIES

If you are emailing your CV as an attachment, you need to make *absolutely* sure that it arrives in the same shape that you sent it in. Word-processing software is inclined to foul up your beautifully formatted document (another reason for using standard fonts), so first send your document to a few friends' computers to make sure it arrives properly. Get them to print it and then *you* should check every detail of its formatting.

The other detail you need to watch out for if you're sending soft copies is the 'Properties' of the file you send. If you have asked friends to look at your CV or if you sought professional help in composing it, that may leave footprints in the Properties of the document. Save a clean copy of the CV on to your hard drive and open the Properties (generally found under the 'File' menu on your word-processing application). Make sure that it is *your* name in there as author and as the last person to save and print the file.

You can avoid all this hassle with layout and footprints by converting your file to the Portable Document Format (filename.pdf) using Adobe Acrobat®. (Some operating systems and word-processing applications have this capability built in now.) This ensures that the file will arrive with exactly the formatting you sent and also that no one can tamper with it – as recruitment agencies are wont to do.

8. CONSISTENT DESIGN PROTOCOL

Establish a protocol for the look and feel of your CV that makes the reader's job easier and stick to that protocol throughout all of your correspondence. Unless you are sending a text-only document (see page 19) over the web or in the body of an email, you have tremendous scope for drawing attention to the important elements of your document using the formatting tools in your word-processing application.

The reader who is scan-reading your CV for the first time is looking at job titles and the organisations you have worked for, and possibly an overview of your qualifications and training. Make it as easy as 1, 2, 3.

Put your **job titles** in bold as they are usually the most important thing to highlight. Put the *organisation names* in italics. When you are delineating training and education, you can continue the protocol – putting the names of the institutions in italics and the qualifications or courses that you took in bold. Here's an example:

CAREER AND ACHIEVEMENTS

<u>August 2008 to Present</u>
Headhunted by *Widgets Incorporated (UK)* as the **Senior Management Accountant**, reporting to the Financial Controller. *Widgets* competes in the blah-blah sector, the local affiliate has a turnover of £XX million and employs 350 staff. Along with the typical analysis, audit and reporting functions, my brief encompasses:

- Line management for 11 staff – 3 Accountants and 8 Clerks
- Development, implementation and updating of all policies and procedures under my purview
- Capital expenditure projects from inception to completion
- Collaboration on key projects – insurance, systems development, stock control

Key Contributions

- Migration from legacy system to SAP – project team member
- Merger, acquisition and diligence activities from time to time
- Conducting training in finance for non-financial management

May 2005 to August 2008

Joined *Fidgets Ltd* as **Payroll Clerk,** reporting to the Management Accountant. *Fidgets* is a London-based manufacturer and distributor of yadda-yaddas. I rose quickly through the ranks following my qualification in January 2007. Progression:

Payroll Clerk	May 05
Accounts Clerk	Dec 05
Accountant	Feb 07
Management Accountant	Nov 07

July 2004 to May 2005

Following four rounds of interviews, *Gidgets Ltd* in Surrey selected me ahead of 250 applicants for the role of **Job Title,** reporting to the Boss Title.

EDUCATION AND TRAINING

INSTITUTION	QUALIFICATION	YEAR
SAP UK	**Project Team Training** **Project Management** **Financial Accounting** **Corporate Finance Management** **Business Programming (JAVA)** **SAP Supplier Relationship** **Management**	2007 & 2008
College name, location	**Masters in Business Administration** Thesis: Implementing an ERP System in the multinational setting	2008
Fidgets Ltd Training	**Leadership Skills I & II** (I was also placed on the internal Mentoring Programme)	2007
Whizzy Mgmt Institute	**Management Development** **Programme (12 week)**	2007
Institute name, location	**Membership Exams (ACA)**	2007
Whoopeedoo *Training Ltd*	**Advanced MS Excel and Word**	2005

Gidgets Ltd Training	Induction Training:
	Time Management/Putting People
	  First
	Presentation Skills/MS
	  Windows & Office
		2004

School name, location	**A levels**	2004

AND ANOTHER THING . . .

Three final thoughts on formatting and design, the first two of which are related.

First, it really helps if you can type, and, second, your life will be immeasurably easier if you can actually use your word-processing software. If you are not already proficient, learn. Computer illiteracy is fast becoming as much of a hindrance and as professionally unacceptable as functional illiteracy. Don't rely on the good graces of others to do this donkey work. With the best will in the world, they won't care as much as you, even if you are paying them. Learn how to type and how to word-process.

The typing part is easy: there are a number of computerised tutorial programmes available that can literally 'talk' you through the training. There are also many computer courses available, but I would recommend that you identify a tutor (your network should be able to help here) and spend a few hours with him one-on-one, learning just those parts of the workings of your machine and of your applications that you actually need to know. You can always top up with another grind later as the need arises. This may cost you a bit more and you won't get a certificate from the process but, in my experience, far too many so-called computer courses are geared towards getting you through the course rather than giving you a clear understanding of, and real ability to use, your computer.

My final thought: have a design professional from your network give your document a once-over. Hand him/her a red pen and invite them to make look-and-feel amendments. You will nearly always get a pearl of advice with this approach.

'At Sony, we assume that all products of our competitors have basically the same technology, price, performance and features. Design is the only thing that differentiates one product from another in the marketplace.'

Norio Ohga, former Chairman and CEO

Chapter 10

DEALING WITH GAPS IN YOUR CV

I suspect that a patchy career history affects a high percentage of people. You know the sort of thing – a bad move followed by a major piece of bad luck followed by another move to an awful company, a lull in the market . . . and the next thing you know, it looks like moths have attacked your CV.

How do you cover off on this problem as you put yourself out there in the marketplace on paper? If you were just given the chance to *talk* to a potential employer, you could probably explain the patchiness away in an instant; unfortunately, you have to let your CV do the talking for you.

In putting your thinking together on how best to deal with problems in this area, start, as always, from the perspective of a potential employer. If you present a piebald CV, what is likely to be going through the reader's head? It will be a rare employer who looks at one of these and thinks touchy-feely, positive thoughts – 'Oh look, an unexplained gap; I'll bet this person took a much-needed career break to volunteer in sub-Saharan Africa and learn many new and exciting skills.' More likely, they will think of dismal, negative possibilities:

- Couldn't hold down a job because of itchy feet, immaturity, or just being some kind of nomadic dolt?
- Burnt out?
- Fired and couldn't get a job?
- Making licence plates as a guest of the state?
- Couldn't get hired anywhere because of a toxic reputation that I don't know about yet?

Naturally, where possible, you want to put a good spin on any and all gaps on your CV, but sometimes that just isn't possible. One hundred per cent honesty may not be your best policy, but full-on lying is rarely going to serve you well either. The world has become far too small (and Google far too pervasive!) to hope to get away with glaring omissions or fabrications about your past. There are two major reasons not to tell a big lie during a job-hunt:

1. If you get caught, your professional credibility will be irrevocably blown and you will, like as not, lose your job.
2. If you do get away with it, you will be looking over your shoulder every day and

may find you have lied your way into a
square peg in a round hole situation to
boot . . .

WHEN, WHERE, HOW?

When do you explain the fissures in your past, and
where and how? I would recommend getting the big
reasons-to-hire-me into the reader's face first.
Typically, your cover letter is the first thing they
read, so you need to move *way* past a perfunctory
'Please find herewith my CV' and get into the meat
and potatoes of why you are the answer to their
prayers – there is a full chapter on this below.

Deconstruct it. Break down the job you are applying
for into its component elements and rate yourself
against the key success factors for the job. If you are
not scoring highly, do yourself a favour and don't
apply. If you are the cat's pyjamas for the job, clarify
exactly why and tell them. *Then* you can think about
explaining how you fell off the planet for nine
months. Twice. In three years.

FUNCTIONAL SCHMUNCTIONAL

The conventional wisdom is that you paper over the
cracks in a gappy work history by producing a so-
called Functional CV (see page 18). This style of CV

highlights your major skills, clustering your achievements and contributions regardless of when they occurred. For example, you may have done a small amount of research work for a radio programme in three different jobs in your past and you are now applying for a researcher role in a major radio station. The functional CV allows you to clump all of the skills and experiences relating to those disparate times into one section of your CV so the recruiter doesn't have to join the dots. In this instance, I would say a functional section on your CV is a good idea.

But, if you're using the functional CV approach to mask a series of gaps in your working history, good luck to you. Because the functional approach is a less common format than the chronological CV, any experienced reader is likely to look askance at your application and immediately start wondering what you are trying to hide. It is for this simple reason that I do not recommend using this format. If you don't provide some sort of chronology or a really good explanation for the crevices, you will be waiting a long old while for an invitation to an interview.

ANCIENT HISTORY

If the gaps appear way back in the ice age of your career and you have had a strong, contiguous career for the last 5–10 years, then you can go for a résumé-style CV and simply leave your early history off altogether, or cover it with a one-liner like: 'I spent the early part of my career in the blah-blah industry, cutting my teeth in junior roles and learning the intricacies of the business.' Alternatively, you can 'cluster' a series of patchy jobs from your past. A typical, no-holds-barred, chronology looks like this:

Jun 04 – Present	**Widgeting Guru**	*Smidgets Inc.*
Jul 01 – Jun 04	**Widgeting Wizard**	*Fidget & Co.*
Dec 99 – Dec 00	**Widgeting Manager**	*Gidgets Ltd*
Jan 98 – Apr 99	**Widgeter**	*Digit Inc.*
Mar 97 – Oct 97	**Widgeter**	*Legit Ltd*
Mar 96 – Dec 96	**Widgeter**	*Hitch It & Sons*
Sep 94 – Mar 96	**Apprentice Widgeter**	*Widgets Inc.*

Fairly patchy, with two three-month and two six-month gaps on there. The one positive in this one is that the individual has stayed in the same industry and has shown steady, if unexceptional, career progression along the way. Why then, are the gaps such a problem? Primarily because, in this day and age, no one is going to leave a job to go to nothing unless they *have to*. Gaps of this nature immediately beg the question: did the individual go or was he/she pushed? And, in either case, why?

For this example, it would be better to ensure that you get to interview, and further, to avoid becoming bogged down in that discussion at interview, by 'glossing over' these downtimes. A résumé coverage of this person's working history, clustering the early years, could be presented like this:

Jun 04 – Present	**Widgeting Guru**	*Smidgets Inc.*
Jul 01 – Jun 04	**Widgeting Wizard**	*Fidget & Co.*
Dec 99 – Dec 00	**Widgeting Manager**	*Gidgets Ltd*
1994 – 1999	**Apprenticeship & Widgeter**	*Digit Inc.*

It's not 100 per cent honest, but there has been continuous employment since July 2001 and most employers aren't going to be too interested in this individual's life before he/she became a Manager. This person would just need to make sure that they covered off the January to June 2001 period with a clean, brief explanation.

One note of caution – if some gung-ho recruiter goes looking for early references, they will probably uncover the gaps, so you'd better have your story straight and it had better be consistent with what those early referees/employers are saying about you.

REASONS NOT EXCUSES

If you have moved job-type a lot, or if you have been taking numerous temporary or contract assignments, papering over the cracks as in the example above is probably not going to be enough. You will need to provide some degree of explanation with each cluster of piecemeal working history. None of these is 'safe' per se, but they are better than nothing, and you can measure the acceptability of your pitch according to your success rate and feedback from your network. So, you can tell your potential employer that you were:

- Considering your options
- Travelling – the 'much-needed career break' approach
- Doing contract work to fund a job search for a more fulfilling career
- Coursework – but you'd better have some parchment to show for it
- Significant (but now resolved) illness
- Carer for elderly relative
- Winding up a complex estate following bereavement
- Stepping back in to a family business at a critical time

QUICK DEPARTURES

These happen and they look just *awful*. We've all seen the scenario – someone got headhunted for a lot more money, but the organisation was like the ninth pit of hell and they ran screaming out of the door after six months. If this has happened to you, the tack to take on it is that it took immense courage for you to do this and to admit your mistake not just to yourself, but also (through your CV) to the market. And what did you learn from this experience? Well, at the very least, I trust that you have checked out the organisation you are applying to now with a *microscope*, so there are going to be no unpleasant surprises on either side this time.

Be very careful that you don't bad-mouth that hellish previous employer, no matter how much they deserve it. Any interviewer listening to your vivid descriptions of the lake of fire in the finance department of Company X will be thinking, 'I wonder what this person will be saying about this company (or me!) in a few years' time?'

THE LONG VIEW

A couple of gaps on your CV are not a bad thing. The clumsy cover-up is a bad thing. Getting caught in the clumsy cover-up is a *really* bad thing.

Remember, a linear, un-chequered, *Little Lord Fauntleroy* CV can be perceived as being boring, staid, predictable or overly conservative. Look at the CVs of some of the household name CEOs and entrepreneurs. Along with the headline-making successes, there are gaps, failures, firings, educational holes, false starts and retracing steps along the way.

Let me close by saying that finessing your way out of a 'patchy' CV is simply not always possible. If you have no choice but to admit an unfortunate truth about a gap, you may have to take a significant step backwards to prove your stability (and your worth) to the market again. I would have to say that one common strand I come across in the vast majority of cases like these is that the individual is, to some extent, floating along. If you are working to a plan for your career, these patchy episodes tend not to arise and, if they do, you can see them for what they are and quickly take corrective action.

The factor that no potential employer wants to see is *repeated instances* of this kind of behaviour, because that means you keep sticking your hand in the fire and learning nothing each time you do it. Take your licks, learn your lesson and get back out there!

'Our great democracies still tend to think that a stupid man is more likely to be honest than a clever man.'

Bertrand Russell

Chapter 11

SUMMING IT UP – THE COVER LETTER

If your CV is an advertisement designed to get you to an interview, your cover letter is the first second of that advertisement, which will either cause the reader to sit up and pay attention or to reach for the remote control to change the channel . . .

Your cover letter is the first thing about you that any employer sees and will therefore form the basis of her initial impression of you. A well-presented and well-structured piece of writing will always dispose the reader favourably towards you, so give the cover letter the attention it deserves.

A cover letter should neither be a restatement of your CV, nor should it be a cursory 'Here's my CV . . .' note. All too often, cover letters are just dashed off and are nasty, generic documents. We all get 'Dear Occupant' junk mail in our homes and our inboxes are stuffed with spam – and everybody *hates* it. Well, hey, what a surprise – employers feel exactly the same way about 'Dear Sir/Madam' or 'To whom it may concern' at the top of a cover letter. Spelt the person's name wrong? Bye-bye! They've just been promoted and you wrote to them under their old job title? Welcome to the bin!

There is no excuse for sloppiness of that kind. Find these basics out and get them right. Whether your letter is in response to an advertised position or part of a cold-call process to an organisation that you would love to work for, it needs to address three things – why you are writing to them; what you have to offer; what you would like to happen next – in three succinct paragraphs.

How hard could that be? Well, in today's competitive job market, just as there is no such thing as a 'one size fits all' CV, you need to take time, and be careful and attentive with your cover letters.

LAYOUT

You should create some stationery for yourself. No one expects you to invest in engraved letterhead on heavy linen paper, but a crisp and distinctive header and footer will always look more polished than a same-font-throughout, hastily typed cover note. Try putting your address at the top, centred in a different font. Tie this in with your CV – whatever font you have for the body copy there is your font for the text of the letter, and the font/style that you used for the headings in your CV can be your letterhead.

Here are some examples:

> ROWAN MANAHAN
> HOUSE NAME
> STREET ADDRESS
> TOWN
> POSTCODE

> Rowan Manahan
> House name
> Street Address
> Town
> Postcode

Or, you can right justify it and make it very discreet:

> ROWAN MANAHAN
> HOUSE NAME
> STREET ADDRESS
> TOWN
> POSTCODE

> Rowan Manahan
> House name
> Street Address
> Town
> Postcode

Your footer should be a line extending across the whole page with your home phone, email and mobile phone details underneath:

T: (CODE)123 4567 • E: rmanahan@yourisp.com • M: (CODE) 234 5678

This is crisp, neat and something *very* few people bother to do. What does it say about you? 'I am polished, I am professional, I pay meticulous attention to detail, and I am not run of the mill.'

Make sure you date your cover letter and, if it is in response to an advertisement, put a subject header (plus any reference number) up at the top:

ROWAN MANAHAN
HOUSE NAME
STREET ADDRESS
TOWN
POSTCODE

10th Month, 201X

Mr Joseph Brown
His Title
Widgets Incorporated
Address
Town
Postcode

RE: Operations Manager (ref no. 123 XYZ)

Dear Mr Brown

Further to your advertisement in the *Paper Name*, I am applying for the above position . . .

GETTING IT RIGHT

Once again, put yourself in the shoes of the person who will be reading this document and question the value of, and impression cast by, every word that you include. Every aspect of your CV and accompanying letter needs to be targeted:

- **Right industry** for your qualifications/training and experience (they may also be looking for use of appropriate terminology)
- **Right organisation** for you (public service vs. private sector, indigenous vs. multinational, relaxed vs. uptight, people-focused vs. overtly profit-focused)
- Most importantly, sent to the **right person** – the person who is capable of actually giving you a job

BANG BANG BANG

Your opening paragraph says that you want the job and why you are suitable for it 'My extensive track record of accomplishment and contribution in the area of Operations Management renders me a suitable candidate for the vacancy in your team.'

Your second paragraph expands upon that, delineating in broad strokes those elements of your qualifications, training, experience and personal attributes that pertain to the job. You can do this with a series of bullet points or in *very* punchy sentences. For advertised positions, you can frequently reverse-engineer from their stated list of requirements: duration of experience, qualification level, must-have skills and nice-to-have extras.

Your third paragraph should say something along the lines of: 'I enclose my current *Curriculum Vitae*, which will expand on the above. I trust that this will be satisfactory to you and I look forward to discussing my candidacy further with you at interview.'

You can sign off 'Yours faithfully' if you have never spoken, 'Yours sincerely' if you have (see below), and 'Best regards' if you know the addressee quite well. Leave a space for your signature and print your name:

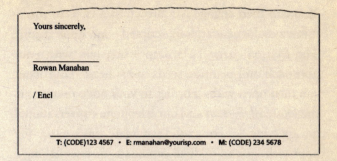

Yours sincerely,

Rowan Manahan

/ Encl

T: (CODE)123 4567 • E: rmanahan@yourisp.com • M: (CODE) 234 5678

WARMING UP A COLD CALL

An unexplained piece of correspondence arriving on someone's desk is never as powerful as a piece of correspondence that has some context, expectation or recognition value. It is a great help if the reader can put a voice and background to your letter/CV, so you should always consider making a quick call to better position yourself in his mind:

> 'Mr Brown? Rowan Manahan is my name. I saw your advertisement in the *Daily Blah-Blah* and I'm interested in the position. I just wanted to get a sense of how the Operations role fits into the Widgets organisation chart. I currently report to the Managing Director of my company – to whom does the Operations Manager report there at Widgets?'

You can then engage Mr Brown in a two- to three-minute dialogue (carefully scripted – see Approaching The Market, page 121), impressing him with your approach and planting seeds in his head. Your letter can then open with, 'Further to your advertisement in the *Daily Blah-Blah* **and our telephone conversation,** I am applying . . .' For a solid candidate, this is a sure-fire approach. For an oddball candidate, or one making a transition into a new career, it is even more essential.

Sometimes, with the best will in the world, you just *can't* convey succinctly in writing the reason why you would be a good candidate for a job. A picture paints a thousand words? Well, a chat is always going to paint a better picture than a cover note. The body of a good, tight cover letter will be 200–300 words in length or roughly 1½–2 minutes of talking time. If you have done some thinking and role-play in advance, you will always be more engaging and convincing on the phone (or better yet, in person – but these appointments are almost impossible to get) than you will be in writing and you will be able to say more and expand upon your points in a way that you just *can't* in writing. So do your research and make that call!

SPECULATIVE LETTERS

What if you desperately want to work for Widgets Incorporated but they haven't advertised for a very long time and your research is not giving you any sense that there are likely to be positions arising in the near future?

First port of call – your network. How is business going at Widgets? Are they on target? Growing versus last year? Holding their margins? Who are the new entrants and threats in their space? Have there been any regulatory changes in this sector in the recent past? Globally, have there been any significant changes in the way that Widgets does business? New faces? New strategic approaches? New products/ services launched? Mergers or acquisitions that have affected the business?

Second port of call – the HR department in Widgets. Talk to the most senior person you can get to and determine:

(a) are there jobs coming up?
(b) in what department(s)?
(c) how do they usually fill those jobs – agencies, headhunting, bounty-hunting, website ads, trade magazine ads, newspaper ads?
(d) who are the players in the department you want to work in?

During the course of this dialogue, you can subtly let the HR person know how well-informed you are about the state of play in Widgets by dropping some of your big pieces of knowledge into the conversation. This is why you need to talk to a senior person – junior HR people rarely have this breadth of knowledge and insight and, as such, they usually are not worth having this sort of conversation with.

Once again, for those of you who haven't been paying attention:

DO NOT write to HR looking for a job.

They have no power to create a position or to decide finally who gets that job. Write to the person who knows what is going on in the relevant department (typically the head of that department) and who can cajole extra money out of the budget to support a hiring decision that he sees paying dividends for the organisation.

From the reader's perspective, speculative letters are the most tedious ones to receive. In many cases, there is a standing instruction to the administrator who handles the post to pass these letters on to HR. So it is highly advantageous if you can position yourself in advance, and the phone is the simplest way of doing this. When your letter *does* arrive on Mr or Ms

Player's desk, it needs to address one thing only – that you are aware of a difficulty/problem/issue facing the organisation and that you are (or have) the solution. That approach *might* get you a 15-minute meeting.

> 'Letters are expectations packaged in an envelope.'
>
> Shana Alexander

Chapter 12

LITTLE BOXES – APPLICATION FORMS

Employers in certain sectors just *love* application forms and, for the hirer at the coalface, they do have a number of advantages:

- There is nearly always a declaration that you (the applicant) have to sign stating that all of the information given is true, followed by a warning statement from the employer that 'falsification can lead to summary dismissal', or words to that effect
- Hirers can compare like with like more easily by using a standardised format and can get through the tedious business of initial screening more rapidly
- You are frequently required to include information that you would normally omit from your CV, such as: health status or sick leave record; reasons for leaving your current and previous employments; precise remuneration details for each position held (and remember that 'falsification can lead to summary dismissal'). They also typically

require you to indicate month and year for commencement and termination of each employment, which can expose gaps that you might otherwise prefer to gloss over

APPLICATION FORMS – THE ABSOLUTE BASICS

You would be astounded at how many candidates disqualify themselves from consideration by making careless, fundamental mistakes in completing application forms. At the very least, you should do the following:

- Get extra originals or make copies of the form for trial runs
- Very carefully check through the instructions section and any instructions in the accompanying letter – employers can be very specific (e.g. block capitals in black ink)
- Read all the questions on the form thoroughly, making notes on a pad as you go. Do this at least twice
- Draft your preliminary answers on paper and then sketch out a draft on one copy or a spare original
- If you are working with an online form, copy and paste the questions into a Word® document and draft your answers there

- Many application forms now specify a maximum word count for certain answers – pay very close attention
- When you are finished, read it through several times and note any improvements that you might make. Then read it again with the employer's hat on and make sure that you have addressed all of *their* principal concerns. Now is the time to canvass opinion from your network
- Fill in the original. In many instances now, you can do this online. If it has to be handwritten and your calligraphy is not up to scratch, get a friend with really nice handwriting to do it for you
- Compose your covering letter (see page 103)
- Proofread everything carefully – get friends (preferably literate ones!) to help you do this to ensure accuracy
- Copy everything for your records
- Deliver by registered post or by hand and get a receipt – if it's an online delivery by email, you will have proof that you sent it, if you're just hitting the 'Submit' button on the company's website, you'll just have to hope for the best . . .

SPECIAL SECTIONS THAT CAN MAKE A DIFFERENCE

Some of the boxes on a standardised application form do allow for a measure of individuality.

The extra information/supporting statement section

This is usually the last section to be filled on the form and it is one of the few boxes in which you can really express yourself well, so it is vital and can make all the difference to your application.

Tailor each word that you include and make sure that every sentence highlights your potential *value* to the organisation. Human beings hiring other human beings buy *benefits*, not responsibilities. Your level of responsibility in previous jobs indicates your maturity and reliability, but many other candidates will have broadly similar experience. Responsibilities provide reassurance to the reader; the achievements and contributions that you made on the job are what make them want to meet you . . .

For a paper application form, try and stay within the confines of the box provided – impress the reader with your tight writing style. For online forms, stick within the specified word count.

Make certain that you have included everything that you would normally put on a CV.

The interests section

Keep this section as short as you would on your CV. You can use it to identify yourself further with the personal attributes the employer is looking for. Employers look to the interests section of a CV or application form for a number of reasons:

- To see how you round out as a person
- To allow for some 'relaxing' questions if the interview gets too hot and heavy
- To identify conflicting interests that may make large demands on your time and interfere with your ability to meet deadlines, stay late at work, etc.

For both your CV and any application form, you should consider including current interests under the broad headings identified in The Profiler (see page 66):

- Professional
- Physical
- Cerebral
- Social
- Altruistic

OK, you now know what kind of job you would like and you have your written representation of yourself all ready to go. Where and how are you going to send it? Your **route of entry** into your desired sector is vital and that's what we'll cover next.

> 'We think in generalities, but we live in detail.'
> Alfred North Whitehead

Chapter 13

APPROACHING THE MARKET

Job-hunting is not like it used to be. You can't just open the Appointment pages of your broadsheet newspaper-of-record and find the job of your dreams. In many instances now, the first time you hear about a job is after it has been filled. This has been christened the 'hidden jobs market' and it is frustratingly like an iceberg – with only a small percentage of the available jobs visible above the waterline.

If you are about to embark on a job-hunt, there are many strands you need to consider. Three of the most important foundations in your process are:

1. hunting smartly by reverse-engineering
2. the route (or routes) of entry you use
3. taking as much active control of your job-hunt as possible

1. REVERSE-ENGINEERING

Take it from the end and work your way back by reverse-engineering your hunt. If you have identified a list of companies you would like to work for, you need to find out what methods they use to find talent – what websites, agencies, newspapers, etc. Then build your approach to them on that basis. Phone them, talk to them – don't ask for a job – just establish *how they hire*. Even a low-level person in HR should be able to help you with this. Then you can mix-and-match your approach to optimise your chances.

Good poachers are good poachers because they know where the best spots are and they concentrate their traps and lines in those spots. A focused day's effort using the *Yellow Pages*, the internet, and working the phones will fill in a lot of the blanks in your knowledge of where, and how, to hunt for your next job. You must start at the end and work your way back, otherwise you are hunting blindly.

2. ROUTES OF ENTRY

Job vacancies arise every day – this is ubiquitously referred to as 'market churn'. People retire, resign, die, take career breaks, get hit by trucks, go on long-term sick leave, decide to work part-time, get promoted, get transferred, get fired or get kidnapped by Martians and disappear off the face of this planet *every day*. No matter how sick your sector is, no matter how sick the economy is, there are *always* jobs out there; you just have to find them. And that means spadework, shoe leather and sweat – whoever coined the axiom that job-hunting is a full-time job was right on the money.

The major routes of entry are:

Cold-calling

Otherwise known as spraying bullets into the trees, hoping to hit something. It can work and *does* work, but the return on invested effort is very low and the sheer volume of applications you have to send out precludes any kind of meaningful research or groundwork. If you have the discipline to limit your efforts to companies you would *really love* to work for, experiment with this route.

Newspaper/magazine advertising

This was a vital route in the past, but is becoming less valuable now. The Appointments sections in newspapers and trade magazines are getting thinner and thinner, reflecting more sophisticated approaches by companies looking for talent. In my experience, companies use advertising of this nature:

- Because they have to – it's a legal requirement that the position be advertised (e.g. teaching posts)

- For PR purposes – to let the market know how well they are doing
- As a matter of last resort – because they have exhausted every other means of finding the perfect person to fill this role
- And sometimes, simply, because they lack the imagination to hire people through any other route

No matter why a company advertises in this manner, your problem is that you will be up against every bozo and bottom-feeder in the market jamming their CV into the HR department of the company. With that kind of signal-to-noise ratio, the odds for your CV, no matter how good it is, are not stacked in your favour. Nevertheless, people get hired via this route all the time, so you have to make scanning the important dailies, magazines and trade journals an ongoing part of your job-hunt.

Recruitment/placement agencies

Placement agencies do have some excellent positions for certain sectors, but many people make the mistake of regarding them as a 'friend in camp' as they pursue their job-hunt. It is important that you don't lose sight of their real agenda – agencies (and headhunters) make their money by selecting the best candidates for the vacancy in their client's organisation and putting those candidates forward with the *minimum* of effort and time spent. Every phone call they make, every email and letter they send, is money out of their pockets. So, if you are in any way unsure what you want to do next, or how to approach the market, don't expect to get any help from this quarter.

Some guidelines for dealing with agencies:

- Position yourself crisply, leaving no doubt in the agency's mind that you know what you have to offer, what you want to do next and are committed and focused on this career path. If you haven't yet *firmly* decided on your career path, keep away from agencies until you have.
- Make them work for their money. Extract the maximum information from them that you can, every time you have contact with them.
- That being said, expect to have to work hard at the relationship. If you call them, don't expect them to call back. It can be a pleasant surprise if they do, but most won't.
- Deal with players. Find out who the directors or owners of the agency (or local branch of

the bigger agencies) are and deal directly with them – they will care more about the business and provide better service than younger, less-experienced members of staff might.

Many employers are using multiple agencies to find the best candidates now. Register with a number of them and don't be afraid to play them off against one another – you may be able to glean a few extra morsels of information with this approach.

Headhunters

You are sitting at your desk one fine day and the phone rings. The caller introduces herself by saying, 'My name is XXXX, I work with Blah-blah Executive Search and Selection and I was given your name as a possible candidate for CEO of the Universe. Is this a good time for you? Can you speak freely now?'

Wow, flattering or what? As you would expect, these calls don't happen very often, nor do they get made to people below a certain salary threshold; but, boy, is it nice when they do happen! How can you *make* them happen? Getting on to a headhunter's radar scope is not easy; the top-end players in this arena receive *massive* numbers of unsolicited CVs every day, most of which they ignore. You need to take a very sophisticated, lengthy and probably expensive, approach in order to put yourself on the map in this way.

If you are going to approach these people, your CV needs to be really top-notch (even more so than if you are sending it to a placement agency). It needs to reek of professionalism and point to a rapidly progressing career with an unfailing level of contribution and accomplishment throughout. Then they just *might* call you back.

Always preface any contact you make with a headhunter by phoning first. Do a bit of research to find out who handles your sector and do some background on her. If you are in her bracket and have the right credentials, you won't get the brush-off; if you are in any way a stretch of her imagination, you are going to have to do some very careful positioning to get your foot through her door.

The internet

For many job-hunters, the internet has transformed the way in which they approach the market and, for most employers, the internet has likewise trans-formed the preliminary stages of the recruitment process. But no more than that. The internet is not a short cut to a new job, nor is it a magic pill that will, in some way, prop up a shoddy approach to job-hunting on your part.

It *is*, however, a marvellous resource for finding jobs that you might otherwise never hear about. And it is a very important development in the way in which job-hunters can research potential sectors or employers in advance of applying. This is (of course!) a double-edged sword – now that information is so freely available, employers have far higher expectations of candidates in the early stages of screening and selection. So, if you have Luddite tendencies, you are going to have to work much harder than your competition to glean information about the market and the organisations that you want to work for. Far better to make the investment in time, effort and money and embrace the best that technology has to offer the modern job-hunter. In the vast majority of jobs, you will need to have these skills anyway, so start acquiring them as soon as possible.

Your approach to the net, and what sites you register with, will be determined by the sector you are in and, more importantly, by the way in which your target companies hire (see Reverse-Engineering, above). Your starting point is to use the web to research the major players in your sector, confirm their local presence in your *Yellow Pages* and find other, lower-profile companies alongside them. Once you have built your target list, you need to track their websites – with particular reference to the 'News/Investor Relations' and 'Careers With Us' pages.

There are myriad job sites and boards out there and you will need to establish a presence on a number of them as you pursue your hunt online. But what if the companies you want to work with don't use those sites? There's an old adage that there is a thin line between fishing and standing by a river like an idiot. Once again, I say – good fishermen fish where the fish are.

I constantly encounter frustrated clients who are generating little or no response from their online efforts. They see Widgets Inc.'s logo on a job site but never get called for an interview with Widgets Inc. 'Well, did you call Widgets Inc. to find out if they're still using that job site?' I ask. 'More to the point, did you ask someone in Widgets Inc. if they still use that job site to advertise positions in your area of expertise?' There's every possibility that Widgets were given a freebie advert on that site five years ago and used it to hire one person in an area completely unrelated to your desired area of expertise.

Don't stand on the shore like an idiot, because the internet is a wide, deep, fast-flowing and pretty much *endless* river! Find out what bit of the river (if any) the fish you are looking to catch gather in and drop your line in the water there.

Networking

Once you get past entry-level or graduate positions, this is the single most important route into the market. I suspect that this is for anthropological reasons – because human beings are, as a species, wary of total strangers. Despite the fact that 55–60 per cent of middle-ranking jobs are filled through 'some level of personal contact'[1], people shy away from using their network for job-hunting purposes. Most people who resist using this route cite the 'crassness' of calling upon friends, family and colleagues to help them with their job-hunt, or they decry it as 'nepotism'.

I say again – human beings simply do not like dealing with strangers. If I can hire someone who is in some way a known quantity to me, I will generally pick that person ahead of a total stranger. This is not nepotism, this is not the old school tie, this is just human nature.

[1] You can check that number for your locale by calling outplacement and career management companies from your Yellow Pages.

It also makes economic sense. If I stick my head into the canteen and shout, 'Does anyone here know anyone who has skill X?' I'm going to get some referrals and, if I'm lucky, find someone who has skill X and who is being vouched for by one of my staff. No newspaper advertisement. No finder's fee to a recruitment agency. No management time wasted ploughing through dozens of CVs. Quick, easy, cheap and, if I'm a skilled interviewer, effective. I'm only going to go beyond that way of hiring people *if I have to* and, more often than not, I don't have to. So, unless you are plugged into my extended network in some way, you will never hear about the opportunities that arise in my company.

Employers will use this route first and foremost, and anyone in the career management or outplacement business will tell you it is the most productive route of entry into the market. (Interestingly, you will rarely hear that advice from HR people or from recruitment agency personnel – I guess because it would be akin to a turkey voting for Christmas.) So, with no apology, I tell you to get out there and start networking. If you find the whole concept unbearable, then restrict your forays into this arena to research and perhaps getting a tip-off if a position is going to arise in a target organisation. There is nothing worse than opening the newspaper and seeing someone's grinning mugshot in a company announcement of a newly filled job that you would have loved to go for . . . except that it wasn't advertised. Build (or resurrect!) your network and get it humming if you have a job-hunt in your immediate future. Initially, this isn't about anything more than getting back in touch and starting to share information. *Share*. You cannot be a parasite in this activity; the relationship must be symbiotic.

Let's say you meet an old boss for a quick lunch. Your side of the conversation:

> Hello, nice to see you.
> How are things with you?
> Pleasantries, chit-chat, lots of careful
>   listening.
> I'm thinking about making a move.
> I've noticed X and Y and Z happening in
>   the market.
> What do you think? [more careful listening]
> Thanks a million, lots to think about.
> Talk to you soon.

Send an email the next day – 'great to see you, thank you as always for your time and your ideas'. And then follow up! You'll be doing lots of reading and research while you are job-hunting. If you see a titbit that might be useful or interesting to that person, send it along. If you catch a lucky break, let them know – and thank them again. Don't plague them, badger them or stalk them, but do keep in touch.

Here's the key thing, unless you have a very close relationship with that old boss, he/she is unlikely ever to say, 'Give my brother-in-law a call, he'll sort out a job for you straight away.' Modern networking doesn't work like that – rather, it's about having the inside track, and winning through better information. That old boss is much more likely to say, 'You should have a close look at Widgets Incorporated. I heard from a pal who works for a supplier of theirs that they are expanding their operation and that they're going to be looking for people.'

Your old boss can't do that unless she: 1) remembers you; 2) knows you're on the lookout for a new job; and 3) currently thinks well of you. If you are not actively seeking out these old contacts, your alternative is to sit passively by the phone hoping that someone has somehow *telepathically gleaned* that you would like a new job . . .

The idea of networking seems to be something that makes a lot of people's skin crawl. In the 21st century, I have gently to say three words to you:

Get. Over. It.

Make your networking about information and ideas rather than big favours, and most people won't have a problem with it. Reassure them – you're just trying to find out what's going on, to get the lie of the land; you're not going to whip out your CV ten minutes into the conversation and beseech them for a job . . .

Over the years, I have written extensively about the how-tos and wherefores of networking. If you're unnerved by the prospect of approaching the market using this route, or have no clue how you should begin, I recommend picking up a copy of *Where's My Oasis* (Vermilion, 2004) and you'll also find some thoughts on my blog.

ACTIVELY MANAGING YOUR JOB-HUNT

In a tight market, you are probably going to have to cast your net quite a bit before you land a fish. In simple terms, you can either **go wide** or **go deep**. Going wide means firing off dozens (or even hundreds) of cold-call letters and CVs to companies and hoping that your envelope arrives on the right desk, saying the right things, at the right time. It *can* work, but that's an awful lot of stamps to lick . . .

Going deep means building a shortlist of companies you would really like to work for and compiling a CIA-style dossier on each one of them. This is hard work and time-consuming, but it greatly increases your chances of getting the rightly phrased CV on the right desk at the right time. Think about it – we've all been disturbed at dinner time by a complete stranger wanting to sell us telephone or broadband services. You can picture them, sitting in front of their computer with a headset on, reading off the script. And it rarely, rarely works. We all feel the same way about junk mail in our letterboxes and spam in our inboxes. Well, that is *precisely* how most job-hunters are perceived by employers.

Stop applying for just any job and start thinking about applying for the handful of jobs you would really like to be doing. Focus the bulk of your time and effort on those. You can always have another strand running simultaneously – registering with a bunch of recruitment agencies, for example.

The other things you need to do in managing your job-hunt are: stay on top of it; and keep the ball in your court wherever possible.

Staying on top of your hunt

The most common frustration I hear expressed by

job-hunters is 'lack of control'. If you put a simple mechanism in place to stay on top of all your job-hunting activity, you will feel much more in charge. At the most basic level, this means a diary. Not just to keep track of your appointments, but also to keep track of your activity. If you called Agency X today and they said they would get back to you, note the conversation and put a reminder to yourself to contact them again in four days' time.

If you are conducting a wide or a deep-but-long hunt, a paper-based system is going to be quite cumbersome. If you are using a computer for word-processing and email, you can also start tracking a lot of your activity on there too. Outlook and the other email packages have diary systems with tasks, notes and reminders built in. Very handy.

There are also specialist online career management tools. The best I've seen is Jibber-Jobber (www.jibber jobber.com) and it allows you to track everything – for free. You can also upgrade to a paid service, with premium features, for just a small amount a month. Well worth checking out. The advantage of being online like this is that you can share experiences and hear how other job-hunters are faring – what tricks they have discovered, little nuggets of information, etc.

Keep the ball in your court

Another problem with this 'lack of control' issue is that most job-hunters are essentially passive in their approach to the market. Stay in charge and keep the ball in your court. Don't send off a CV with 'I look forward to hearing from you' at the bottom of your cover letter. Write 'I will call your office early next week' instead and then make sure you follow up. We've all waited by the phone after a 'don't call us, we'll call you' situation – whether in job-hunting, dating, dealing with an insurance company . . . Keep the ball in your court!

Job-hunting is not rocket science, it's much more about perspiration than it is about inspiration. An organised, persistent, plugged-in job-hunter is far more likely to succeed than his passive, hope-for-the-best counterpart. As children, we were told, 'Don't keep all your eggs in one basket', but, for most adults, we have no choice – our career is our sole revenue stream and all the eggs are in there. So treat the basket with the respect it deserves and stay in control where you can – because no one else cares about those eggs the way you do.

'In preparing for battle I have always found that plans are useless, but planning is indispensable.'
General Dwight D. Eisenhower

Afterword

Beautiful people get hit on all the time. After a while, the language must get very familiar:

- You're so beautiful . . .
- You're so handsome . . .
- You have great hair . . .
- Wow! Those eyes of yours! . . .
- I love your style . . .

The same holds true for beautiful employers. I bet that, if you conducted a word search on applications to Google, the words **exciting, successful, innovative, dynamic, leader** and **great/amazing/awesome** (delete as appropriate) would appear with monotonous frequency. Operative word: m-o-n-o-t-o-n-o-u-s.

So, you've just spotted a supermodel in your neighbourhood. You engineer a meeting in the local vegetable shop. Your basket is filled with carefully selected, sure-to-impress, organic produce. Now, I profess no expertise on the dating game, but I can assure you that opening gambits that include references to her beauty are not going to do the trick for you. No matter how original you think your approach is, believe me – she has heard it all before. You are drowning in her eyes? Ho-hum. You can't believe how luminescent her skin is? Yaa-aaaawn! Her innate grace and poise? Yeah, what-ever!

And the same would hold true for any other celebrity figure, of either sex.

You have to find out what the person you want to woo is interested in. You've got to use your eyes, your ears and your mouth in proportion. You've got to observe the response to your gambits closely. And, maybe on the second date, you can make reference to some unique characteristic, quality or physical attribute that she (back to our supermodel here) hasn't heard a thousand times before. By the way – all of this assumes that you really are head-over-heels interested in this person for who she is . . .

Jean Giraudoux was wrong: 'The secret of success is sincerity. Once you can fake that, you've got it made.' If you have to be anything but authentic in your personal relationships or in your professional relationship with a current or potential employer, it is not going to be a happily-ever-after story. Think about that as you woo that employer. Don't tell

Google how innovative, fast-moving or world-beating they are – what I refer to as the 'You're so big and bwave and stwong' approach – they *know* all that and, no matter how you phrase it, you are going to sound like a naïf or a lounge lizard.

Research. Network. Read. Listen. Think! And then tell them what you genuinely feel about them. Put at least some of your heart on your sleeve. What will working for these people mean to you? Why should the supermodel or movie star in your industry entertain your advances? What makes you so damned special?

That is the Ultimate CV . . .

'A charlatan makes obscure what is clear; a thinker makes clear what is obscure.'

Hugh Kingsmill

Appendix 1

CV THESAURUS

HEADINGS FOR THE SECTIONS OF YOUR CV

Profile/Professional Profile/Overview/Summary/At a Glance/Thumbnail Sketch

Core Competencies/Key Skills/Skillset/Principal Skills/Notable Skills

Key Achievements/Major Contributions/Track Record

Career to Date/Career and Achievements/Professional Progression/Career and Accomplishments/Relevant Career Details/Work Experience/Professional Background

Education/Qualifications/Education and Accreditations/Education and Training/Professional Development/Training

Publications/Presentations/Research Interests/Selected Publications

Professional Memberships/Professional Associations and Development

Extra-curricular Activities/Outside Interests/Interests/Hobbies/Pastimes

Contact Details/Contact and Personal Details

References/Referees/Supporting References/Professional References

DESCRIPTIVE TERMS TO USE ABOUT YOURSELF

Professional/Conscientious/Specialised/Meticulous/ Disciplined/Responsible/Reliable/ Efficient/Diligent

Strong/Adept/Sound/Effective/Successful/ Thorough/Accomplished/Well-developed/ Above average/Confident

Excellent/Exceptional/Outstanding/Superior/ Highly developed/High capacity

Innovative/Creative/Diverse/Inventive/Original/ Resourceful/Ingenious/Imaginative

Strategic/Proactive/Clear/Astute/Measured/Cogent/
Incisive/Shrewd/Coherent

Flexible/Adaptable/Open/Versatile/Accommodating

Trusted/Well-regarded/Reputation gained
with/Respected/Valued/Esteemed

Competitive/Ambitious/Progressive/Tenacious/
Market-driven/Results-driven/Goal-
orientated/Performance-focused/Determined

Proven/Demonstrable/Track record in/Comfortable
with/Familiar with/Adept at/At ease with/Full
knowledge of/In-depth knowledge of/Skilled
in/Confirmed/Verified

Successful/Consistent/Seasoned/Highly
experienced/Effective/Senior/Dependable/Unfailing

Committed/Motivated/Highly
motivated/Dedicated/Staunch/Loyal/Enthusiastic/Keen

Tangible/Concrete/Substantial/Material/Significant

Diplomatic/Sensitive/Tactful/Judicious/Subtle/
Prudent/Perceptive/Discreet

Blue-chip/World-class/Industry leader/Market leading (*all of these would refer to the companies you have worked with*)

XXXXXX-focused (*e.g. Customer-focused, Quality-focused, Sales-driven, Target-orientated, Results-focused*)

Think very carefully when you include descriptive terms about yourself. Are these words what you *think* you are, what you *hope* you are, what you'd *like* to be – or are they what anyone who knows you will spontaneously say about you? If you are going to use this kind of language, it needs to be an honest representation of you, but it also needs to be verifiable – assume that the reader is going to 'ask around' in your sector about you and describe yourself on that basis.

THE SCOPE OF THE JOB THAT YOU DO/DID

My remit included . . .

My purview . . .

Core responsibilities included . . .

Highlights: (*followed by a pithy, bulleted list*)

Overview: (*followed by a pithy, bulleted list*)

My central function was . . .

My brief encompassed . . .

My primary function was . . .
I was tasked with . . .

Along with the typical responsibilities of the role, I also had the following brief . . .

My duties included . . . (*be careful – 'duties' as a descriptive implies a relatively junior position*)

TOOTHSOME VERBS

Avoid the passive voice like the plague (see The Senior/Executive CV, pages 46–7). Where possible, you should start your 'what I did' sentences with a good strong verb. It obviates the need for you to write 'I' and, if you present the 'what I did' material in list or bullet-point format, it immediately draws the reader's eye down the list. You will notice that all of the verbs here are in the past tense – this reinforces the sense of accomplishment.

Increased/Grew/Developed/Expanded/Improved/
Raised/Heightened/Enlarged/Broadened/
Diversified/Accelerated/Optimised/Augmented/
Delivered/Produced/Maximised/Accrued/
Outperformed/Accumulated/Overcame/Exceeded
(expectations or targets)/Surpassed

Won/Beat/Succeeded/Achieved/Performed/

Executed/Delivered/Accomplished/Secured/
Anticipated/Compelled/Forced/Precluded/
Prevented/Averted/Impeded

Reduced/Minimised/Diminished/Saved/Lessened/
Halved/Shortened (usually time or lead
times)/Trimmed/Stemmed/Eliminated (usually
waste)/Dispensed (with the need for)/Eradicated/
Curtailed/Obviated (the need for)/Generated
savings/Lightened

Initiated/Started/Began/Launched/Founded/
Activated/Instigated/Introduced/Set up

Developed/Devised/Pioneered/Designed/
Formulated/Originated/Discovered/Conceived/
Generated/Created/Built/Commissioned/Formed
(usually a team)/Assembled (a team)/Staffed/
Established/Installed/Constructed/Planned/
Composed

Instructed/Ordered/Taught/Guided/Tutored/
Coached/Piloted/Mentored/Appraised/Reviewed/
Trained/Upskilled/Cross-trained

Deferred/Put off/Pushed back/
Postponed/Adjourned/Suspended/Extended

Led/Drove/Directed/Spearheaded/Headed/Central role in . . . /Managed/Supervised/ Oversaw/ Presided/Project managed/Coordinated/Facilitated/ Arranged/Organised/Monitored/Controlled/ Assigned/Budgeted/Scheduled/Rostered

Supplanted/Replaced/Displaced/Superseded/ Succeeded/Overtook/Surpassed/Took over from

Represented/Epitomised/Stood for/Characterised/Spoke for/Symbolised/Embodied

Supported/Provided/Sustained/Buttressed/ Strengthened/Fortified/Reinforced/Complied with/ Encouraged/Motivated/Inspired/Assisted/ Stimulated/Released management from/ Lightened (the load of something or somebody)

Worked closely with/Collaborated/Liaised with/Consulted widely/Interacted/Consulted appropriately/Consulted with stakeholders/Cooperated/Worked together with

Analysed/Captured (information)/Examined/ Identified/Probed/Highlighted/Studied/ Diagnosed/Uncovered/Detected/Evaluated/ Defined/Calculated/Researched/Investigated

Sold/Marketed/Brokered/Negotiated/Persuaded/
Influenced/Espoused/Publicised/Represented/
Promoted/Gained approval for/Lobbied/Gained a
foothold in/Broke into

Enhanced/Improved/Developed/Streamlined/
Standardised/Tightened up/Put shape on/
Shaped/Structured/Edited/Reorganised/Updated/
Renewed/Modernised/Redesigned/
Modified/Revamped/Overhauled/Effected
change/Rearranged/Transformed/
Restructured/Changed/Refined/Converted/
Altered/Change managed/Revolutionised/
Simplified/Revised

Disseminated/Distributed/Allocated/Supplied/
Circulated/Spread

Submitted/Posited/Presented/Contributed/Tabled/
Suggested/Urged/Served as/Pitched/Positioned/
Illustrated/Related/Recommended/Advised/
Counselled/Imposed/Steered/Outlined

Transitioned/Moved/Shifted/Combined/Transferred/
Relocated/Redeployed/Repositioned/Shuffled/
Rearranged

Approved/Endorsed/Permitted/Enabled/
Authorised/Empowered/Consented to/Enacted/
Sanctioned/Agreed/Concurred/Gained consensus

Implemented/Brought to conclusion/Consolidated/
Finalised/Resolved/Completed/Concluded/Settled/
Firmed up/Ended

Recognised for/Consistently recognised for/Praised
for/Selected by management to/Singled out to

Gained approval for/Suggested and
implemented/Promoted/Identified the need
for/Highlighted/Mounted a campaign for

Ensured/Guaranteed/Made certain/Leveraged/
Expedited/Gained advantage by/Forced/Eased

Administered/Ran/Conducted/Undertook
to/Processed/Maintained/Fostered/
Handled/Dealt with/Implemented/Enforced

Recruited/Selected/Hired/Interviewed/Enlisted/
Attracted/Drafted/Appointed

Garnered/Collated/Gained/Procured/Purchased/
Acquired/Compiled/Attained/Obtained/Collected/
Extracted/Removed/Took out/Pulled out

Utilised/Made use of/Applied/Exploited/Employed/
Operated/Exercised/Drew on

Mediated/Interceded/Reconciled/Brought solution
about/Brought together/Arbitrated/Unified

Verified/Confirmed/Tested/Checked/Determined/
Authenticated/Traced/Proved/Demonstrated/
Audited/Inspected/Reviewed/Documented/
Substantiated/Reconciled/Corroborated

Restored/Remedied/Mended/Repaired/Stabilised/
Reinstated/Corrected/Returned/Rebuilt/Fixed/
Revitalised/Renewed/Revived/Breathed life back
into/Rejuvenated/Rectified

Interpreted/Translated/Deduced/Deciphered/
Unravelled/Worked out/Solved

Criticised/Assessed/Disparaged/Censured/
Critiqued/Provided feedback on

Protected/Defended/Preserved/Secured/Conserved/

Retained/Safeguarded/Upheld/Thwarted (competitor)/Blunted (someone else's efforts)/Prevented/Stopped/Impeded/Forestalled/Hindered/Obstructed/Avoided/Evaded/Diverted

Decided/Determined (the outcome)/Chose/Took the decision to/Fixed on/Opted for/Elected to (do something)

Specified/Detailed/Stipulated/Denoted/Indicated/Delineated/Itemised/Insisted upon

Forecasted/Foresaw/Predicted/Anticipated/Foretold/Envisaged

Prepared/Readied/Made ready/Set/Made plans for/Laid out

Declined/Rejected/Rebuffed/Refused/Turned down

QUALIFIERS

Adverbs give us more information about the words that we use, typically verbs (he went *quickly* to . . .) but also adjectives (the music was too *quiet* to hear) and other adverbs (*terribly* slowly.) Three *caveats*:

1. Do not overuse adverbs. It gets tiresome when everything you write is qualified in this way. If in doubt, pick a stronger verb and kill off the adverb.

2. It is still considered bad form to finish a written sentence with an adverb – *He went there very quickly*. It reads better as – *He very quickly went there*.

3. Don't use hanging comparatives on your CV – *We completed the project more quickly*. More quickly than whom or what? Advertisers use this technique all the time – *More music, less chatter* trumpets the advertisement for the radio station. More music than whom? Less chatter than whom? Repeated often enough, catchphrases like these become part of our vocabulary, but they are the kiss of death on a CV.

Quickly/Rapidly/Swiftly/Promptly/Speedily/Briskly/Efficiently/Punctually/Without delay

Successfully/Competently/Capably/Ably/Proficiently/Adeptly/Effectively/Responsibly

Cautiously/Carefully/Judiciously/Prudently/Selectively/Discreetly/Tactfully

Consistently/Constantly/Always/Unfailingly

Creatively/Ingeniously/Resourcefully/Imaginatively

Decisively/Resolutely/Definitely/Positively/
Assertively

Flexibly/Adaptively/Changeably

Enthusiastically/Passionately/Earnestly/Keenly/
Eagerly/Intensely/Ardently/Energetically/Vigorously

Slowly/Gradually/Steadily/Progressively

Significantly/Dramatically/Substantially/Radically/
Considerably/Tremendously

STARTING OUT

Try to avoid the perpendicular pronoun 'I' when you
are writing about yourself. Where possible,
avoid writing, 'I moved to Widgets Incorporated
as a Widgeting Engineer'; instead use 'Appointed as
Widgeting Engineer for . . .' or one of the other
phrases below. Repeated use of 'I' in writing is
somehow less acceptable than using the same term in
a verbal delivery. Start your paragraphs with:

Appointed . . .
Headhunted as . . .
Joined XXXX as . . .
Approached by XXXX to become . . .
Invited to join XXXX as . . .
Gained position as . . .
Offered full-time post as . . .
Invited to return to XXXX as . . .

NIT-PICKING

Your spell-checker is not enough. Firstly, it misses lots of correctly spelt but not-in-that-context words (loose and lose, then and than, bear and bare, horde and hoard, from and form). Secondly, I haven't yet come across a computer that has a diplomacy-checker:

- I worked as a Corporate Lesion
- Objection: to utilise my skills in sales
- Reason for leaving last job: the owner gave new meaning to the word 'paranoia'. I prefer to elaborate privately
- Wholly responsible for two (2) failed financial institutions
- Thank you for your consideration. Hope to hear from you shorty!
- I am a quick leaner, dependable and motivated

My personal bugbear is the humble apostrophe. No one seems to know when to use and when not to use these little fellows. Get this right because, if you come across a nit-picker (and we are legion!), your CV could end up in the bin for this very silly reason.

Apostrophes serve two major functions:

1. To indicate missing letters
2. To illustrate the possessive case

People *constantly* get these mixed up!

MISSING LETTERS:

Cannot	becomes	**Can't**
Do not	becomes	**Don't**
You are	becomes	**You're** (*your* means *belonging to you*)
Would not	becomes	**Wouldn't**
It is	becomes	**It's**

POSSESSIVE:

Belonging to that person – **That person's**

I worked there for five years – **I gained five years' experience**

The headlines for today – **Today's news headlines**

The most common mistake is the inclusion of an apostrophe in the possessive **its**. His, hers, its, ours, theirs, yours – these are known as 'absolute possessives' and no apostrophe is required for any of them. If you write **it's**, make *damn sure* you mean 'it is'.

> 'Short words are best and the old words, when short, are best of all.'
>
> Sir Winston Churchill

Appendix 2

That was Then, This is Now

	DAY 1 ON THE JOB	FINAL DAY ON THE JOB
Age		
Marital status		
Number of kids		
Accommodation		
Mode of transport		
Recent qualification		
Recent training		
Recent self-improvement		
Job title		
Company name		
Boss's title		

	Day 1 on the Job	Final Day on the Job
Key responsibilities: 1. 2. 3. 4. 5.		
Number of staff in company		
Direct reporting staff		
Budget I controlled		
Key skills for the job: 1. 2. 3. 4.		
Measures of success: 1. 2. 3. 4.		

	DAY 1 ON THE JOB	FINAL DAY ON THE JOB
Key things I learnt:		
1.		
2.		
3.		
4.		
5.		
6.		
Accomplishments:		
1.		
2.		
3.		
4.		
5.		

'The best is yet to come.'

Frank Sinatra's epitaph

Acknowledgements

If I have any facility with the English language, it's down to Mum, with all the trips to the library and *The Exchange* bookshop in Dalkey and Pop, with his endless refrain of 'Look it up!'

As always, to Ivan Mulcahy without whom . . .

To Julia, Cindy and all in Vermilion.

I started blogging following the publication of *Where's My Oasis?* – a big thanks to all my readers and especially to those who took the trouble to comment or correspond directly with me. You've been a huge source of energy and ideas, thank you so much for sharing.

About the Author

Rowan Manahan has been providing career advice since 1993 and is the founder of Fortify Services, which provides consultancy and outplacement services to the public and private sectors and a career management service for individuals.

Working both with employers on the hiring line and with job-hunters on a daily basis, Rowan has developed a strategic methodology and toolset for job-hunting in the 21st century. He makes his living providing simple, workable solutions to frustrated job-hunters, and the techniques he advocates have proven successful for clients operating at all levels of the organisation chart. He has been variously described as: 'The Career Doctor', 'The Insultant' and 'A Reverse-Engineering Guru', but prefers the simple, understated moniker that he developed for himself while at university – 'Manahan-The-Magnificent'.

Rowan lives in Dublin with his wife, Marie, and his two daughters, Lynn and Jane. He loves good minds, great music, smelly cheese and chop-sockey videos. He is in the enviable situation of bouncing out of bed every Monday morning with a smile on his face, and sees no valid reason why everyone else can't do that too.

Index

Also available from Vermilion:

Where's My Oasis?

By Rowan Manahan

Whether you are changing jobs, going for a promotion or recovering from a redundancy, in today's marketplace job-hunting is for dummies – the smart people career-hunt. *Where's My Oasis?* offers you a one-stop shop for all your 21st century career management and job-hunting needs.

With guidance on career-planning, finding your own strengths, CVs and applications, interviews and much, much more, this book is the definitive must-have for everyone looking to move forward in their career or thinking of changing their life.

£12.99   ISBN 9780091899981

Order this title direct from www.rbooks.co.uk

Also available from Vermilion:

The Body Language Bible

By Judi James

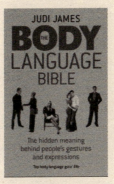

Did you know that flirting at work is all about keeping peace in the office?
Or that shaking someone by the hand is a gesture evolved from ape behaviour?

In her inimitable straightforward style, Judi James unravels the secrets to interpreting our movements and what we are really saying with our bodies, whether consciously or not. She teaches you what we mean with our body language, how to interpret it and then shows you how to get what you want, whether you're doing business, making friends or falling in love.

£8.99   ISBN 9780091922115

Order this title direct from www.rbooks.co.uk

Also available from Vermilion:

Lend Me Your Ears

By Max Atkinson

Professor Max Atkinson is an expert speaker and trainer who has been involved in speech writing for business, politics and the arts for over 30 years. In *Lend Me Your Ears* he uses the findings of recent scientific research combined with the rules of classical rhetoric to highlight the secrets of successful persuasion.

Using extensive research, Max has developed a new and provocative way of looking at speech making, providing the reader with practical and simple guidelines, exercises and tips to improve performance.

£10.99   ISBN 9780091894795

Order this title direct from www.rbooks.co.uk

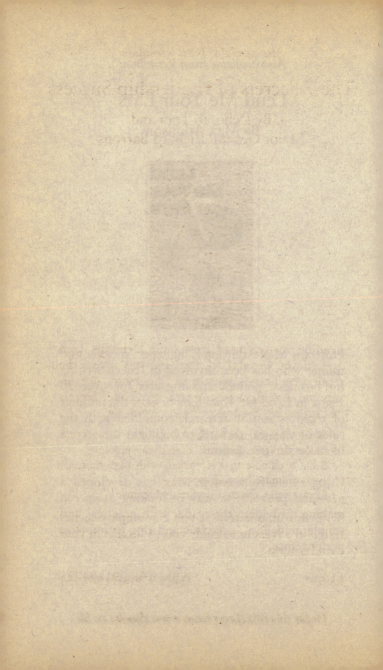

Also available from Vermilion:

The 7 Secrets of Leadership Success

By Deborah Tom and
Major General Richard Barrons

Leading management consultant Deborah Tom and Major General Richard Barrons reveal the modern military's secrets to leadership, organisational development and strategy. *The 7 Secrets of Leadership Success* will enable you to:

- Work smarter, not harder
- Make the right decisions, even under pressure
- Build a climate that is envied, with high morale and committed engagement
- Create agile, effective and united teams

With this unique toolkit you can employ tactics tested in adversity to guide you to success in your own business.

£8.99   ISBN 9780091906931

Order this title direct from www.rbooks.co.uk